the magic of horse whispering
HORSES don't LIE

For Laura,
Best wishes,
Chris Irwin

by
Chris Irwin
as told to Bob Weber

GREAT PLAINS PUBLICATIONS

Great Plains Publications Ltd.
420-70 Arthur St.
Winnipeg, Manitoba
R3B 1G7

The lithograph "Survival" is reproduced
courtesy of the artist, Lynn Kistler

Design and typography: Taylor George Design

Printed in Canada by Friesens

Canadian Cataloguing in Publication Data

Irwin, Chris
Horses don't lie: the magic of horse whispering
ISBN 1-894283-02-3
1. Horses—Psychology. 2. Human-animal relationships
I. Title
SF301.I78 1998   636.1'00'9   C98-920151-1

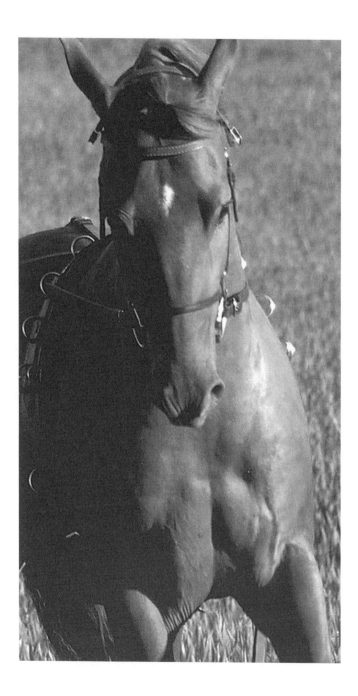

For Anita
Thanks for the dance
of faith and fury
thanks for the silliness
thanks for pushing me
thanks

Contents

11   Preface

16   Beginnings

31   Predator and Prey

41   Being the Better Horse

59   Riding the Wave

71   Training the Rider

81   Character and Consciousness

95   Etiquette

104   Epilogue

111   Afterword

PREFACE

Magic. That's what we've always thought it would take to talk with the animals. And from ancient legends, to fairy tales, right up until Dr. Doolittle, it's one of our oldest and deepest dreams. But today, there is a new generation of men and women who have found, with horses, the reality within this time-burnished myth. They are able to get right inside the horse's head, speak to it, and command it.

Maybe you've seen one of them demonstrate it. Most commonly, these so-called horse whisperers or non-resistance trainers will walk into a round pen with any number of horses he or she has never seen before. With a few gestures and steps, the trainer has the horses pounding around the pen and within half an hour or so, the animals are following the trainer around like puppy dogs with hooves. Often, the ones that come in bucking and rearing and snorting succumb the quickest. And sometimes the trainer even gets up on one of the horses and rides it around bareback. Invariably, the audience is impressed — and a little awed, too.

There's no doubt it is impressive. It's a world away from the muscles and hobbles and ropes that most of the audience is used to associating with horse training. Here, there's no force, no coercion. There's just a trainer walking around the middle of the pen, focused like a laser beam on every twitch of the horse's tail or toss of its head. Now and then he steps toward the horse or backs away from it or flicks a whip or a rope toward its butt. And then — suddenly, gently — there's that horse, following the trainer around, muzzle just over his shoulder like his shirt pocket's full of sugar. Sure, it seems like magic.

Well, it is and it isn't. To the horse, there's no magic here. In fact, it's only because what the trainer has done is logical, not magical, that it works at all. But the logic we're talking about here is horse logic, not people logic. And when people start to learn from and think like horses, magic happens.

You see, horses don't lie. They don't separate how they feel and how they act. The expression "What you see is what you get" could have been coined for them. Whether they're feeling scared, confused, submissive, bold, or just relaxed and confident — and believe it, horses feel all those emotions and more — they tell you exactly where they're at and what they want from you and mean it down to the bone.

Every moment you're with them, they're taking your measure with the accuracy of a creature whose very survival depends on precise readings of its environment. You can't fake it with horses. You'll just confuse them and frustrate yourself if you try. To achieve the results I've just described, you must open your mind and allow your horse to show you how to communicate with the same depth and transparency it has. And that's when the magic starts.

It's magic because what horses need to hear from us is what many of us would like to hear from ourselves. They want us to have a calm, focused assurance. They want us to be consistent. They want us to be both strong and compassionate. In short, horses need us to be our best selves. And by being so sensitive to our self-doubt and fear, they help us find where we keep all our inner betrayals so we can root them out.

So the hard part of horse training isn't really about the horse at all. It's all about knowing who *you* are, while learning about who the horse is, and figuring out who you need to be to bring the two together in mutual respect and trust. To teach your horse to stop resisting and be calm, responsive, trusting and brave, you must first acquire those qualities yourself. You can't just appear to be confident and in control. You must let go of your masks and conflicts and fears and simply *be* confident and in control. Nor can you apply rules you read in a book — even this book. You have to find the parts of yourself that will tell you at a level below conscious thought what you have to do and how you have to act. Everything we can teach a horse, we can teach ourselves. And you may discover that when a horse sees you as relaxed, balanced and centered, so does everyone else. In and out of the horse arena.

This is the first magic. But not only can working with horses restore you to your deepest self and cultivate what's best in it, these wonderful animals can change your attitude to the world around you.

Horses have a fundamentally different worldview from us. In many ways, how they see the world and relate to their fellow horses is the opposite of how we see our environment. Because of that, horses have worked out different ways to get along in the world and with other horses. I believe that we have a lot to learn from their answers. I believe that becoming more horse-like in our awareness of the world and how we achieve our place in it will make us more complete human beings who work and relate well with others, yet know how to stand our ground. What's more, in today's globalized, interconnected world, where we're all affected by the actions of everyone else, I believe that what we can learn from horses is becoming a necessary stage of human evolution. That's the big magic.

Think this is a little airy-fairy, a little touchy-feely for someone walking into a pen to face 1,000 pounds of horseflesh? It isn't. It's as real and down-to-earth as that stuff you muck out of the stalls — just as at the same time, it's as deeply moving as galloping free across the prairie. And as I said earlier, I'm not the first to point it out. Here's what Ray Hunt wrote in 1978: "You're not working on the horse, you're working on yourself." And here's Tom Dorrance, the father of us all: "Riders may want to get an answer to their questions right early — on the surface. I want them to try to *figure out* something; I want them to work at figuring out the whole horse — his mind, body and spirit. Maybe they will figure out what they are missing."

Dorrance called that Holy Grail of horsemanship "true unity." Today's popular culture calls it "horse whispering." Actually, "horse listening" might be closer to the mark, but whatever. It goes back a lot farther than any current fads or fashions. The point is that if you're serious — I mean *serious* — about training your horse, you'd best realize that this is not just a stunt that is used to amaze audiences at a clinic. This can be powerful, life-changing stuff. In fact, that's the only way it works, because the horse is only half the equation. The other half is you. It's hard work. It takes a lot of time and it takes the humility and courage to change the way you think. But it gets results — magical results — for both horse and rider.

CHAPTER ONE

BEGINNINGS

Cowboys call skill with horses being "handy," and for such a simple word there's gotten to be a lot of mystification around it. To hear some people, if you weren't born into a third-generation horse family, you haven't got a hope. And even if you were riding before you could walk, you must still sit at the feet of some saddle-savvy old buckaroo and soak up the Zen of horses like Luke Skywalker and Obi-wan Kenobi.

Well, I didn't. I grew up in St. Catharine's, Ontario, on the little land bridge between Lake Ontario and Lake Erie. We were surrounded by orchards, water and industrial cities. We were almost as far from the open plains and foothills of ranch country as anyone could get. My mom tells me that as a child I was always excited when Mr. Ed came on the television, but I don't remember that and it probably doesn't mean a thing. My sport, believe it or not, was competitive rowing. Mentors? I've learned from lots of people, but mostly I've put things together by watching, doing, and thinking. The point is that handiness is learned, not bestowed. And I can prove it, because that's how I got it.

Eventually, my family did move west from Ontario to Swift Current, Saskatchewan. Swift Current, in the southwest corner of the province, is ranch country and that's where I met my first horse. He belonged to a high-school girlfriend of mine, and I used to love watching the two ride around. Or maybe it was just the girl. Either way, horses were still no big deal to me. Interesting, yes. But I was much more excited about girls, hanging out with my friends and playing my guitar. And that's mostly what I did.

As we got older and left high school, some of my buddies packed up and headed out for jobs, mostly in the Alberta oilpatch. A lot of others went to university for four more years of classrooms on the way to becoming young professionals. Somehow, neither choice felt right for me. So, in 1978, I did what seemed to be the logical thing: I built a snug little winterized camper on the back of an old pickup truck and I headed off to the mountains. I spent that winter roaming ski resorts, soaking up the challenges and beauty of the mountains, and at the end of the season found myself in Whistler, British Columbia. Wondering what to do next, I crossed the border into Seattle. Then, out of curiosity and a vague feeling that I wanted to be around horses, I went over to Longacres racetrack and asked around for work.

I didn't know anything about horses. But I got a job, the same first job almost everyone in this industry gets — mucking stalls. I lived right with the horses, in a cleaned-out stall with a bunk in it. I fell asleep listening to their nickering and woke up with their smell in my nose. And cleaning those tight little box stalls housing big, high-strung thoroughbreds, you can bet I got my first lessons on being around them.

It was clear right away that horses had personalities and moods. Some became my friends and some stayed enemies until the day I left. Most interesting of all: they seemed more afraid of me than I was of them. One day, a horse told me something I didn't understand until years later: when I pressed in on him, he turned his head away from me, then swung his head back around and took a second look when I retreated. I'll return to this later because it's important if you want to understand horses.

Anyway, I learned I didn't mind the hard, dirty work of the horse world. Maybe I got that from rowing — few sports demand more in the way of perseverance and just working your guts out than competitive rowing. But most of all, I learned to love horses — the sound of them eating, how neat it is to come across a horse that's sweet and friendly and willing to spend a little time with you. I caught on to things quickly, and the trainers noticed. Before long, I was walking horses to cool them off after exercise and grooming them after that. Then I got offered a job for a little while at a breeding farm as a trainer's assistant. It was there that I learned more about the care and feeding of horses, as well as necessary skills like how to build a proper fence.

Chris in Whistler, BC, 1980

When winter came, I loaded up my camper truck and went skiing again, and that's what it was like the first while. Eventually, it got so that I was missing the horses during ski season. I starting looking for a job that would keep me around them during the winter, and in 1981, with a little luck and a lot of 20-year-old cockiness, I talked my way into a horse job. Back in Whistler, I convinced the owner of a team of draft horses who gave rides to tourists that I could handle and care for his animals. He taught me to harness them and I was off. There were some wrecks and there were some runaways, but for the most part it was a good winter. I was learning to drive and learning to ride.

The next winter, I went down to Lake Tahoe, Nevada, to visit a friend who was working on the central ranch of a big outfit that ran a string of riding stables and dude ranches. They had hundreds of horses, and I began helping out. Sure enough, I got offered a job. I didn't accept right away, but I did a few months later and that's when things really started to go.

Down in Tahoe, it was 12 hours a day, room and board with $100 a week under the table, but I was apprenticing. I was feeding, grooming, saddling, bridling and riding. I don't mind admitting back in those days it would get rough between me and the horses. What I knew about them amounted to how to hang on, when to stand my ground and when to back off. One thing I did have was soft hands. Maybe it came from playing the guitar, but I always had a gentle, accurate touch on the bit, just as some people can drop the needle on a record right into the groove and some people bounce it across the vinyl.

The main activity at this ranch was taking young, green horses and training them for riding. Although a lot of the guys at this ranch were pretty handy, they'd grown up under the old school and it was harsh on the horses. But there was a farrier there who taught me a lot. John Barnes couldn't read and couldn't write — he'd carve a notch into a stick each time he did a hoof so he'd know how much to charge at the end of the day — but he was really easygoing with the horses and he'd slip me a few choice words now and then.

"A horse has to go forward even to back up," was one John-ism. "When the horse does what you want it to do, then stop asking," was another. John was the first one to tell me to get out of the horse's face, to give the horse some breathing room not just in the saddle but on the ground. He taught me that a horse shows disrespect by turning its butt toward you. I still use his lines in every clinic I give.

That fall, I had an accident that made a big difference in how I came to deal with horses. I was riding a lot, often at full gallop over some pretty rough terrain. That's what I was doing one day, laughing over my shoulder at the guy behind me, when my horse stumbled and we went down. I broke my leg in 13 places. I snapped three ribs and fractured my skull. I spent most of that fall in hospital and the whole winter of 1982 recuperating. The horse I got hurt on wasn't a bad animal — I just wasn't paying attention. So when I got back to work that spring, I started watching horses a lot closer. I realized that there was real danger in this business. The result of my accident was that I was spooked enough to slow down so I could think twice about everything. I started wondering if it was possible to get a little more work done on the ground, to get the horse safer and quieter before I got on. This was an important lesson.

I spent four years at that ranch, skiing in the winter and, in a basic way, training colts the rest of the time. I was literally living among the horses, out in my camper behind the corrals. I worked them all day and at night, I sat on the haystack and just watched them. The horses I'd been with at the track had all been kept in separate stalls, but here on the ranch they were all kept together.

Sometimes, I'd go in to catch a horse that was in a big pen with a hundred other horses and if it didn't want to be caught, I would have to try to separate it from the others. When one horse gets going, they all get going and you end up in there in the middle of a cloud of dust and hooves playing games with the herd. I got so I could see turns coming before they happened. I started to notice the way the horses were interacting. I began to understand herd dynamics, and the natural pecking order of herd animals. At the end of those four years — as long as most people spend getting a university degree — I was getting pretty 'handy.' My approach to horses was still overly aggressive and forceful, but it was coming.

Then, the ranch closed. I took some savings and struck out on my own, buying, training and selling green horses. I did that until about 1989, when I opened a little dude ranch. Unfortunately, rising insurance rates during the mid-eighties eventually squeezed the profit right out of trail riding. That ranch closed too. I took my savings and struck out on my own. Soon I found myself falling in love with one of my first clients as a freelance trainer.

Robin was a sweetheart. She'd been around horses some, but not enough. She was, however, an old hand with natural forces. Robin owned and operated a sailboat charter business on Lake Tahoe. While I was riding colts during the day, she was right across the street, taking tourists out for the sailing experience of a lifetime.

After work, we would get together. Sometimes she gave me sailing lessons but most of the time we worked with her young arab-quarter horse mare. It didn't take long before we were married.

Together with a mutual friend we opened a ranch retreat nestled deep in the Pinenut Mountains of Nevada. We accommodated only ten overnight guests at a time. The facilities were beautiful and the trail riding, in that setting, was awesome. My routine was to maintain the hot tub and the pool, take guests for rides and buy, start and sell colts.

Later, we expanded into a day program, busing up to 200 people at a time from the casinos for afternoon and evening excursions that included wagon rides, horseshoes and barbecues. Sometimes, I would even get up on stage and entertain the guests with a little guitar playing and singing.

The fun only lasted a couple of years. Neither Robin nor I really enjoyed catering to a steady stream of tourists. I was also beginning to feel homesick for Canada. I'd been gone for almost ten years. Even more depressing, I was beginning to realize that I wasn't as deep in love as I thought.

Also, our partner wasn't really pulling his weight at the ranch and soon nobody was happy. Fortunately for us, however, the ranch had become quite well known so it didn't take long to find a buyer.

I went back to starting colts and Robin began exploring a new career in a local art gallery. Pretty soon, I was working 14 hour days, seven days a week in an effort to avoid dealing with our fading love. It wasn't too much longer before Robin and I took advantage of Nevada's quick and relatively painless opportunity for divorce.

Needless to say, after that experience, I really threw myself into work. Down in that country, everybody had a round pen in their yard. They'd use it when they were taking a green horse for its first ride, so the horse couldn't run them into a corner. I had one too, and I began using it as a small space where I could work a horse and teach it some manners. At this point, I wasn't thinking about unity and communication between horse and human. All I wanted to do in those days was to keep working the horse until he didn't want to run away any more, to try and apply what I'd learned on that first ranch.

I had started to develop a local reputation as someone who could be trusted to start horses, to make them safe and reliable. One day, a saddle-maker from the area was watching me work a horse and asked me if I'd ever heard of a horseman named Ray Hunt. These days, Ray Hunt is one of the godfathers of our kind of work, but back then only the cowboys knew about him. I certainly didn't. Hunt was giving a clinic in the area, and when I went to check it out, I realized that, sure enough, we were working along the same lines. At the end of the day, I was introduced to Hunt as the local boy who was handy with horses. Oh, I was cocky. Hunt asked me if I learned anything, and I said: "Sure. I learned I should be giving clinics." To his credit, Hunt threw back his head and laughed and said, "Good for you!"

That's one of the things I like about this business — horse people are straightforward and don't mince their words, and they appreciate that quality in others. Maybe that rubs off from the horses. Just as important, I learned there were other people doing what I was doing, trying not to just beat up on horses but to bond with them. There was a fancy name for it, too: non-resistance training. I had just been calling it "playing horse."

Anyway, things were going well for me. A lot of people were bringing me horses to train. I saw old horses and young horses. I worked with horses for driving, riding and dressage, with owners who rode Western or English style. Things were going well but they were about to get even better.

I was at a show one day when a young woman came up to me with a horse who had some behavior problems. Anita Zdancewiecz was a dressage rider and a professional instructor, but her horse wouldn't load into the trailer. I started working with her horse, and she started coming around to the stable and asking questions about what I was doing. Nobody had ever done this before. I was used to working alone and doing my work more or less on the level of instinct. Now, for the first time, I had to explain myself. Anita would ask me "What are you doing?" and "How did you know when to stop?" and "How did you see that coming?" and would just keep asking me.

She knew a lot about horses — more than I did. She was there every day for a week, watching me work her horse and by the end of that time I was giving an ongoing commentary: "Watch, he's getting ready to relax and stretch," or "Watch, I think he's getting ready to lick his lips now." After years of work and hundreds of horses, I knew intuitively what was going on, I knew how to talk and listen to horses, but now Anita was forcing me to reason it through and explain it, first to her and later to the other English-style riders she knew. For the first time, I was beginning to understand what I was doing. Smart woman, this Anita. I couldn't let her get away. We were married soon after.

That's more or less how I came to learn the basics of what people today call horse whispering. I had a lot more to learn about subtleties. Still do. But as for the horsemanship, *those* are the main sources — watching, listening to people and horses, and putting things together through sometimes painful experience (I've had 30 broken bones along the way). I also took lessons from outside the horse world. Rowing gave me the discipline for hard work and developed the sense of balance any good rider needs. Guitar gave me soft hands. Skiing taught me to work with natural forces, not against them.

By the early 1990s, I began to understand that something was developing that was more important than simply being 'handy' with horses. I'd had considerable success in the industry. I'd won 18 different American national championships with wild Mustangs, both riding and driving. A sweet little Morgan I'd trained was cleaning up in state and regional shows down in Nevada. Plus, I was getting a good reputation with everyone from people at the Calgary Stampede to the renowned dressage trainer Willy Arts. I knew I could continue as a successful trainer. But thanks to Anita, I was now interested in becoming a teacher as well.

Anyone who's ever taught knows it forces you to think harder about what you're teaching. That's what began happening to me. Standing in the middle of a round pen, horses whirling around me like a living, breathing, thundering sacred circle, I had a lot of time to reflect on what I was doing with the horses, what that meant, and what effect it was having on me.

Even back in St. Catharines, I'd always been a bit of a brooding, introspective kid. My home life hadn't been easy. One relative was an alcoholic who belittled and knocked me around quite a bit. Surrounded by lies and evasions and used to living with pain, I grew up full of questions about integrity, authenticity, and worth.

As a kid, in order to answer some of these questions, I first turned to the Boy Scouts. I loved the movement's rituals and traditions, its devotion to honor and doing your best. And on camp-outs, the Scouts introduced me to Nature. I became a leader in our local pack and I still have an old clip from the St. Catharines' newspaper of me at the head of my troop at a Remembrance Day ceremony. All the

Chris (left) standing ramrod-straight in front of his scout troop.

other kids are distracted and goofing around, but I'm ramrod straight, intent on the ceremony and its meaning.

But my time with the Scouts ended badly when a local priest involved with the movement was found to be sexually abusing one of the younger boys. Finding out that the ritual I loved only hid lies and abuse, I left.

I next turned to sports. Rowing was *the* sport in St. Catharines and my longing for something meaningful drove me to do well at it. Very well, in fact — rowing for my hometown crew, we won the Royal Canadian Henley regatta, one of the sport's biggest events. But even this wasn't enough. Standing on the medal podium in front of thousands of cheering spectators, I broke into tears. I had my gold medal and my 15 minutes of fame, but so what? An emptiness still remained.

The doubts continued when my family moved to Swift Current. Nobody was much help, either — they looked at me as if I were crazy when I asked too many questions, or told me to forget that stuff and just get a job. I read a lot. I became a Christian, even undergoing a born-again experience. It still wasn't the answer.

Those were tough days. Despite my music, despite my girlfriends, despite my buddies, I felt beaten up and tired. As Jack Kerouac once said, I was at the bottom of my soul, looking up.

Finally, when I was about 19, I spent a couple of weeks in a monastery in Saskatchewan. Talking to those kind, wise men, I came to understand that my path would be to go off into Nature to look for a kind of healing and work my way into a better future.

That's what I was doing when I packed up my camper and headed off to the mountains. That's what I was doing when I first starting training horses. And that's what I'm still doing as I work my way along the path of life.

By the time I started to teach, I'd already noticed that my work with horses — these wonderful emissaries of the natural world, had introduced me to some qualities within myself that I was finally happy to meet. And eventually, I started thinking about how the things I was doing in the round pen related to what I was doing in life. That circle of thought started to spiral outside myself. I started to make some comparisons, look around at what others have said and experienced, and I believe I started to get a hold on the real significance of what I was doing. Like my horses, my thoughts began to whirl.

But I'll get to that. It's time to talk about horses.

CHAPTER TWO

PREDATOR AND PREY

Horses have been domesticated for thousands of years. It's thought we first began purposefully breeding them and harnessing their strength as long as five thousand years ago on the grassy, open steppes of Central Asia. Only dogs have been with us as long, or served us as well.

We're used to seeing these animals together and when I travel around in horse country, it's a rare acreage or horse stable that doesn't have a dog loping around somewhere. In fact, it's a question I often ask at my clinics — how many of you out there own dogs? Lots of hands go up.

But I don't see so many raised arms when I ask how many have hired a trainer for their dogs. Now, someone in the audience always says "I don't need to hire a trainer to teach my dog his job. He sleeps all day and mooches food like he was born to it." And sure, we tend to ask a lot less of our dogs than we do of our horses (I'm not even going to get into cats).

Still, few people have trouble training dogs to come when called, or stay when told, or not to chew the furniture.

PHOTO: JIM KNELSON

Anita, Chris's wife, with horse Sassy and dogs Nikita and Basha.

Even kids can train dogs to do fairly complex tasks. It just seems to be natural to a dog to focus its attention on its master, which is the first and most important requirement for training an animal.

So if horses have been with us as long as dogs, why are they so much harder to train? To understand this, we need to back up for a moment and look at the big picture. We have to look at some fundamental relationships in the natural world before we start discussing the specific relationship between humans and horses. And when we do look at the larger picture, a recurring pattern emerges.

Nature is full of relationships defined by two seeming opposites that are in reality constantly interacting. The two need each other. One is defined in relation to the other and the spark that animates them comes from the tension and back-and-forth flow of their different energies. Think of day and night, the positive and negative poles of a battery, think of male and female. Eastern philosophers call this principle yin and yang, and consider it such a powerful concept — and so important to keep in balance — that they use it to organize everything from their spiritual practices to their diet. Others call this pattern 'duality,' but I prefer to use the word ' polarity.' Horses are into polarity in a big way. They think in polarities. To a horse, you're either this or that, one or the other, in or out. 'In-between' just creates stress for a horse and they don't understand 'almost.' So is there a polarity between horses and humans?

Yes. We are predators, they are prey. We, like our dogs, evolved to band together in packs to make it easier for us to kill. Horses evolved to band together in herds to protect each other from being killed. Like the ancient symbols of yin and yang, predators and prey both oppose each other and need each other to live and keep their numbers in balance.

This is why it's just wrong-headed to compare training a dog with training a horse. We think like dogs. We're both predators. What makes sense to us makes sense to the dog. But with a horse, all those bets are off. It's harder

33

for us to understand a horse than it is for a man to understand a woman (or vice versa). To begin to open your mind to how a horse really thinks, forget about domestication and forget about all your familiar contexts of stables and barns and riding arenas. Think of a horse as a deer. Think about putting a halter or a bridle or a saddle on a wild deer. Imagine walking into a corral and catching a deer and climbing on its back and getting it under control. That's what is really going on with a horse: a predator is trying to get a prey animal to trust it. Long before we domesticated horses and tried to be their friends — or at least their benevolent jailers — we hunted them for food. The earliest representations of horses, on the walls of Iron Age caves in France and Italy, show them with our spears thrust into their rib cages. We may have forgotten this. Horses haven't.

Predators — which we humans remain despite centuries of agriculture — behave and think in certain ways. Our predatorial mind is fairly linear. We focus our attention on our prey and move directly towards it, concentrating on that goal and shutting out everything around us. We're hunters, after all. If we fail to focus on our prey, our hunt is likely to fail and our survival is put in jeopardy. So naturally, we've learned to focus well. This tendency to goal-oriented, A-to-B behavior is key to what I call predator consciousness. You can see it in everything from the way a kitten stalks a ball of string to the way a hockey player homes in on the opposing net to the way students focus in on the lecturer. It's all about narrowing attention and concentration.

But if predators think like an arrow headed toward a target, prey think like the circles spreading out around the bull's eye. They're not into focus, they're into awareness. A horse is constantly aware of everything that's going on: the rustling of the trees, the movement of a nearby animal, an unfamiliar sound. They're evaluating and interpreting all 360 degrees of the environment around them all the time. They are open to everything that's going on around them because they have to be. Why? Because they know, their DNA tells them, that a predator can come hurtling toward them out of those bushes or from behind that rock at any time. To be prey is to be vulnerable, to be a victim. Think about a woman scared and alone in a dark alley in a big city late at night. That's where a horse is and how a horse feels, all the time.

Our job, essentially, is to kill. Their job, essentially, is to not be killed. That results in two widely diverging world views — quite literally. Predators tend to have eyes placed side-by-side on the front of their heads so their stereoscopic vision can judge distance ahead of them accurately. Prey, like horses, have eyes on the sides of the heads to give them a much broader field of view. But because horses are so familiar to us, we lose track of how very different we are. A lot of the problems between people and their horses are about the humans not being realistic about what they're up against. Like a duck taking to water or a dog chasing a cat, the horse's most basic reaction to a human being is to want to have nothing to do with us. It's in their DNA.

There are important things we can learn here. For example, think about that wonderful, 360-degree awareness that horses live in. Nothing escapes them; they are amazingly sensitive and open to everything life sends. Unlike predator thinking, which drives toward the ultimate goal and ignores all distractions, prey thinking must be aware of all the world around it and be constantly poised and ready for anything. Yet it still has to get on with the vital daily business of eating, interacting with the herd and looking after young. It's being alert and relaxed at the same time, like being the coiled spring and the limp noodle simultaneously. I can best explain it by telling a story that I read a long time ago that has stayed with me ever since. This is how I remember it:

> *In Japan, a long time ago, a young man walked up to a monastery and said to the head monk: "Master, I desire wisdom. Will you teach me?" The head monk, a man named Joshu, accepted the young man as a student and put him to work in the monastery's garden. For days, the student did nothing but pull weeds and dig dirt until one afternoon, when he was bent over a row of cabbages, Joshu crept up behind him and gave him a mighty kick to his backside that sent him sprawling. The student popped up, confused and wanting an explanation, but Joshu said nothing*

and walked on. This happened again and again. The student would be concentrating on the job at hand and Joshu would sneak up and send him flying into the dirt. Gradually, the student changed. While still getting his work done, he learned to stay alert to quiet rustles and shifting shadows around him. He honed his senses, stood light on his feet and remained poised for action even when doubled over pulling carrots. One day, he felt something was about to happen and whirled around. There stood Joshu, about to deliver another kick. "Master," cried the student, "I've been here weeks and all I've done is work and receive your blows! When will my lessons begin?" Joshu smiled and replied: "You have already mastered the first one."

I had to learn this lesson before I could get anywhere with horses. And make no mistake, you won't either until you understand something of this. It's the first thing we have to understand when we start working with horses. It's horse psychology 101.

But when I did learn this lesson, a funny thing began to happen. As I, a predator, started to get in touch with prey consciousness, it started to rub off. Here, slowly at first, is where my thoughts began to whirl. And after a while, not only did I understand horses better, but like Joshu's student I began to glimpse a new kind of balance that I could bring to my life.

We need to understand prey consciousness because that's how horses think and we want to be successful with them. But understanding prey consciousness will teach us other things — things like empathy and patience.

Remember that we're taking these wild creatures that are naturally afraid of us, that have the right to be afraid of us, and we're putting them in jail. Think of that the next time you run in to one of these great, big bad horses that really get you upset and angry because they want to fight you. Think of that woman in the dark alley again and imagine that she's fighting for her life. That's what that horse thinks it's doing. So it's important not to lose track of how much transformation needs to take place for that frightened prey animal to become the confident, trustworthy being that we're looking for. It's a long path to travel and once we understand and respect this, empathy follows naturally. And once we have achieved empathy, patience too follows naturally. I hear all the time when I'm giving clinics about how patient I am with the horse, but where does patience come from? It's the result of understanding and empathy.

It's also learning to turn off the ego. Many people become frustrated when they fail to reach the next step with their horse and it is easy to blame the "stupid" horse. In reality, we're angry with ourselves because we believe that training the horse is simply about showing the animal who is boss. The ego says, "If I can't get my horse to do what I want, then I am a loser." But we have to stop insisting that the horse sees and understands things our way. It just can't. Like being the first to say "I'm sorry" after fighting with our spouse, we have to swallow our predator pride, learn how the horse sees things and speak to it in a language it understands. This is a lesson a lot of men need to learn. I see it all the time — the mighty trainer entering the ring to bring the wild beast to heel. No. What's really happening is that the predator is stalking the prey and the prey is terrified.

I made this realization early on in my life with horses. In fact, it's what bonded me to them. When I walked into that stable at Longacres back in Seattle, I realized that these magnificent thoroughbreds were scared most of the time. The very nature and presence of their captors made them want to run and run, but they couldn't. They were in jail, they knew it, and they didn't know why. Despite their power and speed, these great beasts were victims. They reminded me of myself. I very much empathized with a strong, powerful victim because — in many ways — that's what I was. Even though I was physically big and an athlete, I was running all the time from humanity.

I don't believe I'm particularly unique in this. Although most of us can be very strong in some parts of our lives, there have also been times when we've been made into a fearful, cowering victim. It's tempting to simply suppress those memories and try and forget they ever happened, but that's not the way to deal with our fears. Just as we want the horse to forget its fear and turn towards us, we must also face what scares us. Whatever we teach the horse we can also learn ourselves, and coming to terms with prey consciousness will be the first step on the road to overcoming our own victimhood.

Most of us can use a little more awareness, empathy, patience, and humility in our lives. But that's only the first step. We've barely begun to whirl. Once you start to understand how a horse thinks, you can start to influence its actions. And there is a way to do this, a way that will leave the horse doing your bidding out of respect and trust and the certain knowledge that you are acting in its best interest. If you want true control over your horse, you have to convince it that you are the better horse. And that's what we have to talk about next.

CHAPTER THREE

BEING THE BETTER HORSE

There's a trick I like to pull whenever I give a lecture on how horses think. It gets everyone's attention and wakes them up right off the bat, but it also makes a point.

I borrow a watch with a second hand, start timing, and then ask the audience, "What's the point of studying horse behavior? Why are we doing this?" Now, these audiences are usually composed of riders, trainers, horse owners, vets, breeders and other horsey folk. They're a pretty tuned-in bunch, and it doesn't take long before I'm getting answers like communication, respect, building a relationship, loyalty ... all good answers and worthy, rewarding goals in themselves, but all still only means to an end.

It usually takes about a minute before I hear what I want, and I usually have to do a little coaching. The word I want to hear, the word that sums up our goal with the horse, is "control." Whether you're a rider or driver or a vet wanting to handle the horse smoothly, this is about control.

The problem with control starts in those 60 seconds the audience takes to figure out what it wants. Horses live

in the moment: right here, right now. They don't rational-
ize and stand around waiting for us to be clear about what
we want. As I've said before, they don't like ambiguity. So
as we look deeper at the reasons why horses do the things
they do, always remembering that control is our goal, this
is going to become more and more a study in our short-
comings, not the horse's. Understanding equine behavior
often amounts to understanding human behavior and why
we are unable to get what we want. If you think you want
to change the horse, what you really need to change is
your approach to the horse.

I'll give you an example, a simple problem in cause
and effect. If you've got a horse that keeps bucking you
off, you're probably asking "How can I get my horse to
stop bucking?" That's understandable — landing on your
duff in the dirt is no fun. It's always tempting to attack the
symptom instead of the disease, and not just in horse training, either. What you should be asking is "Why is my
horse bucking?" Maybe the horse is scared, defiant, hurt-
ing, or simply bored. To get to the root of the horse's behavior, you need to learn to look at things as the horse sees
them. You need an open mind and a willingness to change.
There's a good chance that the horse's problem stems from
something you're doing. Fix whatever it is — and each of
those problems I mentioned require radically different
solutions — and you'll fix forever the undesirable behavior that stems from it. That is true control, and it starts
from within you.

To learn and develop this control, we have to return to the predator-prey polarity. In the last chapter, we discussed how predator and prey behave differently in their environment. Now we'll look at how they behave differently toward each other. And the central question in any pack or herd is who is going to be the boss, and how is that going to be determined.

Every social group has some way for some individuals to dominate others. If it didn't, no-one would be in charge, no decisions would get made and there wouldn't be any social group. In predator-land, challengers work out who's going to be the leader by trying to immobilize each other. Think about those nature documentaries on wolves: there's the alpha wolf, flipping over a challenger in the pack and holding him still with his teeth around his neck. He's saying, "If you move, I'll kill you. That makes me the boss."

The other wolves show their submission to the alpha wolf by rolling on their back with their feet in the air and their bellies exposed, a position in which they are essentially immobile. But you don't even have to move beyond our own species to see how predators dominate each other. Look at two kids wrestling. One will get another into a hold and keep him there. "Say uncle," he commands. If the other kid does, he's admitting he can't break the hold. He's been dominated.

With prey, it's completely different. Here, movement is the key. The most natural and necessary thing to a horse is forward movement. Horses move from place to place as they graze. Movement is a big part of their mating ritual. They need to move forward to eat, they need to move forward within the herd's pecking order to establish breeding rights. And because horses are so paranoid, the instinct to flee and run for their lives is never far from their thoughts. Everything about staying alive for a horse involves forward movement. I can hardly stress this enough: horses need to go forward all the time.

In fact, if I had had to boil down a horse to its psychological essence, it would be this: a victim that needs to move. So while predators establish dominance by seeing who'll back down, prey do it pushing each other forward. The horse says: if you want to dominate me, you do it by slapping my butt and making me go. That's why horses fight the way they do. When two stallions are rearing up against each other, what they're doing is seeing who will turn tail first and allow the other to push him forward.

This has deep implications for how we handle horses. Too often, when we want to control a horse, we attempt to stop it from moving. This violates the horse's deepest nature. And to make matters worse, we usually stop the horse by attempting to control its head and neck. That may seem natural to us, but as far as the horse is concerned, predators always go for the neck because that's where they make the quickest kill. Remember, we're predators and horses don't trust us to begin with. So when we come in and behave in a manner totally against their nature and right in line with that of their natural enemy, we're going to create fear, not trust. Our entire approach to the horse has been to stop it, confine it, put it in a box, hobble it and tie it up. Then we take it by the head and say "You will be mine."

Our own feelings about control make things even harder on the horse. Control is an emotional issue for people in all their relationships, whether it's between husband and wife, parent and child or boss and employee. Often, we bring our excess stress and problems with control from these other relationships into our relationship with our horse. Imagine someone with a very stressful job, heading out to the barn after work. The horse, already nervous because it can't move freely, sees this: a big predator, full of stress, coming toward his head. Yikes.

So how do we dominate a horse in a way that's natural to it? The same way another horse would — by pushing it forward. We do this by using one of the things predators and prey have in common. Both people and horses like their personal space. In the round pen, we can exploit this — just as another horse would — to push a horse forward and ultimately dominate it. If we step from the center of the pen into that space around the horse, aiming for the barrel just behind its girth, we create pressure on the horse to move in the opposite direction. It's just like an inflated balloon flying out from a finger pushed into it.

However, it's vital to remember that horses do not like to be pressured from the front. That's what predators do. That's how you create fear, not trust. So to give the horse a forward push that feels natural to it, approach from the rear. As I always say in my clinics, to control a horse's mind you must first own its butt. On most horses, there's a spot right behind the rib cage that's like a button that says "Go." To get a horse moving around the inside perimeter of the round pen, that's where I walk toward, and this is how the game I used to call "playing horse" begins.

The first time I played horse for real was down in Tahoe. The horse was Quincey Top Cat (I called him T.C.), a two-year-old liver chestnut quarter horse. T.C.'s curious, intelligent look caught my eye when he came in with a shipment of colts to the ranch where I was working. He was the first horse I ever bought with my own money.

I'd trained a lot of horses by the time I met T.C., but with him I wanted to try something different. This was the spring after my big accident, so first of all I wanted to take it slow and careful. I worked some long, hard days on that ranch and in the evening I was often too tired for more muscle work on my own horse.

Mostly, however, I just wanted to change my ways. My horse work back then was pretty rough and aggressive. I didn't mind getting violent with a horse and, in fact, I kind of liked the adrenaline rush. But I knew in the back of my mind what I was doing when I was strong-arming some poor colt was unloading a lot of rage and hurt from my past. I didn't want to, I didn't mean to, but that's what I was doing and the catharsis made me feel a little better for a while.

What I chose to do with T.C. was a little different. With him, I wanted to bond with one of nature's greatest creatures and do it without a fight. So I decided to just take it slow and make some time to play with him. I was in no hurry to get on him — I'd been riding colts all day — and I'd just get in the round pen with him and walk around, watching, listening and reacting. Hour after hour, day after day.

Without really knowing what I was doing, T.C. and I eventually joined up. We never had a bad moment together. With T.C. I got a taste of what it felt like when a horse gave its heart to you. It felt really good and it felt really healing, and it made me want more. By that fall, I knew that it was time for me to leave the ranch and strike out on my own to explore what T.C. and I found together.

One of the first things I learned was that once this game is under way, it's crucial to stay on top of it all the time. You always have to move with the horse. If I push a horse forward and it trots away and increases the gap between us, I'm not pushing that horse any more. That horse is running away from me. It thinks it's winning and it's not going to learn the respect for me that I want it to have. If, however, I push too hard on the horse and constantly close in on it, it's going to create fear when what I want is trust. The balance has to be just right, based on what the horse is telling me.

Remember, a horse is a profoundly physiological being, by which I mean that its mind and its body are deeply linked to the point of being one thing. Unlike humans, it's just not in a horse to pretend. When you read a horse's body language, you are quite literally reading its mind. A horse is constantly giving off signals about what it feels, whether it's anger, defiance, fear, boredom, fatigue, relaxation or submission. To know how much pressure to apply, you must learn how to read these signals instantly and learn to respond appropriately — that is, as a horse would. It's like a dance, even though one partner has two feet and the other has four.

To gauge the right amount of pressure and read the horse's response simply takes experience and dedicated observation. I can give you some hints and start you off, but I can't tell you how to do it and that's not really my goal here, anyway. Still, it's worth going through the body of a horse, reading it like a book's table of contents, if only to demonstrate the rich emotional vocabulary in the lift of a tail or the line of a back.

Since I've already said the way to a horse's mind is through its hindquarters, let's start there. A tail tells all kinds of tales (sorry). Puckered right down against the croup and the back of the legs, it means apprehensive. A swishing tail signals agitation. Stiff and pointed up, that horse is excited. If it's just hanging light and loose, the horse is calm. What's under the tail can convey a message, too: a little manure dropping out can signify a tense, suspicious horse is starting to relax. Or in another context, it can mean you're literally scaring the crap out of it.

A horse can send you even more important messages with its butt. When one horse turns its hind end to another, that's a big insult. It signals a complete lack of respect, as well as defiance and aggression. It's like flipping you the finger. Same thing with the hind legs. If they're kicking out, the horse is saying: Screw you. The tail, the butt, and the hind legs can all work together, too. They can signal everything from mild disdain to outright contempt.

If you want a horse to respect you, don't ignore any of these gestures. Ever. Ask yourself this: if you let a horse give you its ultimate sign of disrespect, does it make sense to the horse to think of you as dominant? No. In fact, the horse thinks the opposite. So when you try to ride that horse, the horse won't buy it. It won't necessarily buck you off, but it's always going to be testing you, questioning your authority and never automatically doing what you want. All kinds of behavior problems start here, with a rider that hasn't properly taught respect from the very beginning.

Moving forward along the body, the horse's barrel can also tell you what the horse thinks of you. If the horse is leaning against you on the ground, or against your inside leg while you're riding, the horse is invading your space and challenging your control. The horse will use its shoulder to do the same thing.

As well, somewhere in the front of the barrel right around the girth is a line I call the equator. Behind that line, you're in control. You can push the horse forward and dominate it. But the horse knows where that line is too, and an aggressive horse will try to keep you from getting behind it. A horse that keeps turning in to you or pushing against you or being aggressive with its head is saying "If you don't go back there, you don't win." It's like a bouncer at a nightclub, saying "Sorry pal, you don't even get in the door."

The horse's head says other things, too. If the head is up, the horse is saying something's wrong. It's worried or concerned about something, or it's challenging another horse. Or you. If the head is lowered and staying that way, that's likely saying it's submissive — but submissive out of fear, not trust. If the horse holds its head level with its back, then bobs it down and back up, that's the best signal of all. The horse is bowing to you. It's saying "You're the boss."

Again, the horse will use its head to challenge you. People always think it's cute when a horse nuzzles its head right up to you, but unless you've invited that attention that horse is deliberately invading your space. It needs to learn respect.

There's more, much more. If the horse's front legs are even, that's a calm, stable position. One leg forward means it's restless and ready to move. The ears will tell us all sorts of things: back means something (hopefully you) has got its attention; pinned down is angry; pricked forward is distracted, intent on something in the far distance.

Ears that are constantly moving around, like an equine radar dish, are the sign of a relaxed horse tuning in to the environment around it. We need to watch the face, too. Does the horse have a frozen, stiff look? Again, it's scared. A relaxing horse will blink, roll its lips around, flex its nostrils, maybe blow out a little snot.

With all these little messages — and myriad others as well — a horse is telling us what our attitude toward it should be. If the horse is defiant, maybe it needs a little more forward pressure to be shown who's boss. If it's relaxing, it could be time to reward and encourage it by backing off. One thing you'll learn for sure the more time you spend around horses is that they have almost as many ways of challenging unwelcome authority as people do. Like a teenager rebelling against its parents, they can fight you aggressively, by running away, rearing up, or pressing in against you. Or they can fight you passively, by being evasive, stubborn or just plain lazy.

To understand what the horse is telling you and how strong the message is, all the signals have to be considered together and your response to it has to be appropriate. If your horse is calm and its body language is speaking gently, you don't want to rile it up with sudden violent or abrupt gestures. That's like shouting in the middle of a quiet chat.

Equine body language has a subtle vocabulary of great range. I'm still learning it and I doubt that any human learns to read a horse's body language as well another horse does. But you can learn it well enough to first dominate the horse, then teach it to respect and trust you on its terms, not just on terms of fear and intimidation.

Let's imagine we're back in the round pen. We're pushing a horse by moving into his space and pressuring his Go button. At first, it's a contest. The horse doesn't

PHOTO: JIM KNELSON

Chris "playing horse" with two mares.

want to be dominated, or doesn't think you can do it. So it resists, maybe by moving in to your space. Meanwhile, it's tossing its head at you, tail held out rigid. You keep the pressure on, herding it forward, dominating it relentlessly, always absorbing everything its body is telling you. When the head comes down and when you start to see other signs of relaxation, you back off and give it a little more space. You keep the horse moving forward, but not so aggressively.

Finally, when you think the horse is admitting defeat, when its head is low and its movement is relaxed and loose, you take a couple steps back toward the opposite wall of the round pen and let the horse come up to you. At this point, it'll turn. If it points its butt toward you as it turns, you haven't won yet. Tap its hindquarters and get that pony moving again. Dominate it some more. But if it doesn't, it's acknowledging that you're the better horse. It'll lower its head and bow to you. It'll follow you all over the pen and watch you like you're the most important thing in its life. You've given all of yourself to the horse, and it's giving its own trust and spirit back. I've done this thousands of times, just with me and the horse or in front of a crowd, and I never get tired of it. It's a beautiful experience.

This kind of work between a horse and trainer pays immediate benefits. A lot of a horse's behavior depends on its confidence in the handler. Quite often, you'll see a horse sail over a jump with its trainer that it wouldn't go near with its owner. Same jump, same horse. But if the rider doesn't have the respect and confidence of the horse, that horse won't jump a speed bump. Confidence in a handler begins with establishing that herding reflex. The horse must feel it's being herded by a better horse.

Now, being dominated and controlled is not foreign or cruel to a horse. Horses dominate and control each other in the wild. It's natural and even necessary to them. To some extent, it is also natural to a lot of human males. That's why the dominance part of horse training can come easy to us (and the gentling part is something we men have to work at a little harder).

Many women, on the other hand, are socialized to think dominance is always bad. They think of horses and they see loving and nurturing and grooming and caring for their horse. Those are wonderful things. But you don't want to ever lose track of the essential fact that *one* of you is going to be the boss, and that it's going to take some show of strength to boss around 1,000 pounds of frightened animal.

In the horse whispering world of Hollywood and of fiction, a lot people think that if they just understand how the horse thinks, and talk quietly enough, all you have to do is go work the round pen for 20 minutes and you've got a best friend for life. It's a nice concept, it's romantic and sometimes it does actually work like that. But most of the time, you've got to get tough. Passive, non-assertive people don't usually do well with horses. Strength — measured appropriately, in a language they understand — is as much a part of handling horses as is empathy.

Get this part right, and the horse will thank you for it. After all, the higher a horse is in the herd pecking order, the more responsibility for the other horses it has, the more challengers it has to fight off and the more stress it carries. It's a great relief to find someone stronger and more dominant who can take care of him for a change.

In fact, learning how to compete using prey consciousness has a few useful lessons for we predators. When humans compete with each other, it's very adversarial. One wins, the other loses. One gets a massive ego boost; the other is crushed, pinned beneath the alpha wolf or bankrupted by the sharper businessman. Horses compete, too — that's what's happening in the corral or the round pen — but they don't seek to vanquish their opponent. They compete to find their proper niche, to find out how they're all going to live together in the herd. Horses have worked out how to compete without causing the fear, pain, and distrust that we go through because in a herd, the horse that loses the battle is not regarded as a victim. In fact, in prey consciousness the loser is actually empowered because it now acknowledges a stronger horse that will look after it. Horses know that after any contest of wills, they must still all live together in the herd. They compete in a way that makes that possible for them — a way that offers us a model of how we can earn our own rightful places in society while strengthening its fabric instead of tearing at it.

The lessons don't end there. You may be strong enough to establish dominance, but you also have to be consistent enough to keep it. Horses, like kids, need consistency. They don't think in terms of 70 per cent or 80 per cent. Either you are the boss or you're not. You need zero tolerance for disrespect, and that's just the way horses think. That's not to justify going in there and being abusive. What you do is respond appropriately, according to the level of their disdain. If I walk by a horse and it stomps its foot and throws a kick out at me, I'm going to give it a good whack on the butt. But if I'm grooming a horse and I get a little swish of the tail, I'll simply give it a little tap, just to let it know I'm aware of what's going on. You have to measure your response.

But don't ignore misbehavior. That sends an ambiguous message, and horses don't understand ambiguity. This ambiguity is why most people have trouble with their horses. One day we're really sharp as a hawk and not missing anything, the next day we're letting things slide. Horses would rather we not let them get away with anything, because then they know the rules. Otherwise, behavior erodes very quickly.

It's a refrain I hear it all the time: "My horse was great when I bought it." Let me say it again. You have to learn to monitor the body language 100 per cent of the time. Every single moment. There is no cruise control. You must retain focus, for the horse has got nothing better to do than to wait for your mind to wander. People want their horses to be like their cars and computers and all their other toys, complete with on/off buttons, but it just doesn't work that way.

We began this chapter talking about control, and how, human ambiguity and indecision gets in the way of that. Now that we've got that horse circling the round pen, being herded and dominated in the way it's familiar with, we need to let our thoughts circle back to where we came in. It's time to consider how our own minds enter the equation.

Horses don't lie — they always tell the truth with their bodies. There is no separation between what a horse thinks and what its body says. People, on the other hand, bluff and pretend and hide. We learn to pretend interest in small talk, to play social games and tell white lies. We're taught to do it from our earliest age, the first moment mom or dad tells us to stop fidgeting in church and act like we're interested or insist we respond politely to people we feel like yelling at. We've even made an art form out of faking what's in our heads and pretending to be someone else — it's called acting.

Altogether, you might say the ability to be less than forthcoming with our thoughts and feelings is almost a requirement of civilized life. We've gotten pretty good at it, and so, of course, we try it on our horses. People go in to work their horses to show them who's boss when in reality, there's a big question mark in their own minds as to whether they really are. Sorry. You won't fool the horse. Remember, horses are prey animals, they are finely and intensely attuned to their environment. They can spot a faker before he or she even opens the gate. The human has to learn to speak confidently with his or her own body language. And ultimately, this means that confidence can't be an act. It has to be real. This kind of quiet, unshakable faith in oneself isn't easy to learn, but it can be done. We'll talk about what that learning takes a little later. For now, it's enough to know we need it — and that once we have it, it stays with us no matter what we're doing.

So now the circle is complete. To train and work with calm, focused, confident horses, we must acquire these qualities as well. Everything we do with the horses we must also do with ourselves. And as we've seen before, what we learn with our horses will ripple out into the rest of our lives.

Now, we have to take those circles, stand them on end and learn how to ride 'em.

CHAPTER FOUR

RIDING THE WAVE

Everything in this book keeps coming back to circles: the swirling thunder of horses circling around me, the 360-degree circle of the horse's awareness, the herding of a horse in the round pen, the ripples that spread out within us from what all this has to teach. This shouldn't come as a surprise; nature abhors a right angle and is full of cycles and circles. Horses come to us from the world of nature — I sometimes think they were put here to teach us about it — and thinking in terms of circles and arcs and curls is often the best way to understand them. Take the way they move.

Forward motion in a horse starts in the hindquarters and it rolls forward like a wave on the ocean. The hindquarters in a healthy horse are smooth and round and powerful, and the energy they create surges and cycles forward through the barrel, through the shoulders — more roundness — along the neck and breaks like a wave at the head. I can't emphasize that back-to-front, circling flow of energy enough. When you say "Go" to a horse, that word becomes like a stone thrown into a pond, sparking a wave of energy that just keeps moving forward.

Once this is understood, it has profound implications for how we ride a horse. We don't want to get in the way of that forward energy. We want to ride that wave, like a surfer rides a wave in the ocean without disturbing it. And more than that, we want to control and direct the energy of the horse like a dam controls and directs the flowing energy of a river. I know the metaphor is mixed, but I like to think what I'm trying to do on horseback is riding the wave into the dam.

Before we get there, though, we have to backtrack a little. In the last chapter, I described how horses win respect in the herd by driving each other forward from the rear. Humans have to do the same thing if they want the respect and attention of their horses. Control their butts, and their hearts and minds will follow. This doesn't stop once you get into the saddle. In fact, it's even more crucial. Riding is like squeezing a tube of toothpaste: to get the most out of it, you can't start near the top. In practical terms, what this means is that we have to learn to guide and communicate with our horses pressuring our seat, hips and legs into the barrel of horse. We can't, as too many riders try to do, simply use the reins in our hands.

Perhaps the problem starts with the fact we're so used to our cars and trucks. Turn the steering wheel, the front tires twist at the desired angle, the chassis follows smoothly along. It's a natural reflex to think a horse turns the same way — pull one rein, turn the head and the body comes right along with it. This — as anyone who's experienced a horse that refuses to turn no matter how hard the reins are yanked — is not the way it works. Think, instead, of a fish. They turn by bending their whole body through their midsection, all the time powering themselves along with their tail. This is also how a horse turns naturally, by bending through the barrel, and it's how a horse should turn with a rider in the saddle. It seems like a basic concept, but I'm convinced that the significance of bending is one of the least understood aspects of riding. And it's one of the most important: if A in horsemanship is "go forward," B is for "bend."

How does the rider initiate that bend? The same way he or she communicates with the horse in the round pen, with subtle weight shifts and body language. In the last chapter, we talked about how we can push a horse forward to dominate it by applying pressure, that is, moving into the space around the horse's hindquarters. Now we have to return to this idea and get a little bit more specific and a little more physical.

Obviously, once we're in the saddle we can't really get to the hindquarters. We could persuade them with a whip, but that only says "forward" and we need to do more than that. Fortunately, there is a way. At the horse's girth, starting just behind the rib cage and moving forward to below its shoulders, are a series of spots I call "buttons." They're in a slightly different place on every horse, so you have to go looking for them, but once you find them they are the secret to creating that natural bend that will allow you and your horse to develop the agility of a fish in the water.

One button controls forward motion. Press that button with your heels or legs and that tells a horse "Go." There's another button just ahead of that one that says "bend." A little pressure here will cause the horse to bend out, making the pressing leg the inside leg of a turn. A little further up yet is a third button behind and below the shoulders that will also cause the horse to move away from the pressure. You can use this button to finish off the turn you started with the second button: press the second button to create bend through the barrel and initiate the turn; then move to the outside leg and press the third button to push the horse's shoulders into the turn and finish it off with help from the hands on the reins. That outside leg is like following through with a golf swing or a tennis racquet.

Note the sequence here: the turn starts from the barrel, moves into the shoulders and finally the neck and head. The purpose of the reins is not to initiate a turn but to assist in supporting or maintaining and balancing a turn. We wouldn't be balanced in a left turn if we allowed our horse to look right. So we can use the left rein, not to pull left, but simply to not allow the horse to look right.

Power and control in a horse always move from back to front. So many people try to turn a horse from its head. That's just riding backwards. Of course, for this to work the rider must have done his or her homework in the round pen.

The rider has to have established dominance. As we've already discussed, horses won't allow themselves to be bossed around by a horse or human it doesn't respect. So if the horse doesn't respect the rider's legs, it won't bend in response to the buttons being pushed. It'll just push right back. The horse's barrel then stays straight or even flexed in the opposite direction going into the turn, and that creates all sorts of problems.

The first thing that happens is that the rider usually pulls harder on the reins, which almost always causes the horse's head to come up. Remember, horses raise their heads when they're fearful or being challenged, and by raising the head you've just created the stressful state of mind that goes along with it. And that's not all. Raise the head and you consequently lower the back, which is a stiff and awkward way for a horse to move. That means the ride for you is more awkward, which will probably make it harder for you to keep your balance, which makes the horse even more stiff and nervous, which will probably make you hold even tighter on the reins, which is where this whole vicious cycle begins again until the rider gets off and says "This horse just won't turn." But it's not the horse's fault. The rider hadn't won enough of the horse's respect. This series of problems is probably the single most common syndrome in riding. I see it all the time.

Turned properly, however, the horse stays balanced and supple. The head stays down and the back-to-front transfer of power is smooth and strong, like a stretch of rapidless river. Anything the rider does wrong is like a rock in that river, churning up what should only be rushing smoothly forward.

Anita jumping Sassy through a field of oats.

Now, think back to that surfer, poised on the edge of a wave. The surfboard has to be positioned just right: too low on the wave and the surfer gets swamped, too high and the wave will roll right past. The perfect position for the surfer is to find the spot on the wave where the water is changing from a lifting- upward rise to a falling-downward drop. There is a sweet spot on the wave where the water is suspended, where rising energy transfers to falling energy, and this is where the surfer must ride. There is a similar sweet spot on every horse — not so much an up-and-down spot, but a spot where the horse's fore-and-aft, left-and-right motion balances out. With a rider solid, sure and balanced in the sweet spot, communicating clearly in a language the horse understands, the horse's power swells up in the hindquarters, curls up over the barrel and shoulders and breaks over the neck and head. This is riding the wave.

So far, I've only really talked about the legs. What about the hands? Well, I've already mentioned the role they have in maintaining — not creating — a turn. But they also have a much more important function. Think back to the second half of that mixed metaphor I drew at the start of this chapter. Now that we're riding the wave, it's time to build the dam. And that's where the hands come in.

As a river flows into a dam, a reservoir of water grows behind it. That reservoir has many uses, but the one we're interested in involves power. The dam, holding back a lake of water from its natural flow, is collecting a reservoir of power. The hands on the reins and the bridle of a moving horse do a similar thing. At the same moment, we tell the horse "Go" with our legs, we also create a little tension on the bridle. We're asking the horse to create more forward motion, but we're not allowing it to go any faster. This creates pressure, as if we're taking the horse's energy and compressing it. We create a little resistance and a little pressure and like the dam and its reservoir, we let out only as much of the horse's energy as we desire. Using the reins to build this dam and gather a reservoir of horse power is called "collection." It's a subtle thing. I'm not suggesting you pull back on the reins. Just as the dam never pushes back against the river, the hands should never impede the forward flow of the horse.

Collecting the horse requires no backward pressure from the hands, just a firm grip that closes and anchors itself all the way back through the rider's body, deep into his or her spine. Hands that are collecting horse power are like the floodgates on a dam that open one way only. They can be wide open, partially closed or barely ajar, but they will never swing past the center of the door frame and slam the horse in the mouth.

Done correctly, collecting a horse gives you much greater control over it. It's a little bit like gearing down a sports car. The car stays at the same speed, but in the lower gear the engine revs much faster and creates a lot more torque the driver can use to power through a corner or quickly accelerate.

Riding as I've just described — controlling direction from the barrel with your legs and using the hands to finish turns and collect power — allows you to shift from being a reactive to a pro-active rider. A reactive rider is "behind" the horse, constantly reacting to fix problems, trying to fix mistakes and regain balance. This rider tries to control the horse from the head and is likely to be scrambling from one problem to the next, just recovering from the last awkward maneuver when it's time to enter the next one. It doesn't sound like much fun, and it isn't. Pro-active riding begins with being "on top" of the horse, maintaining balance with no need to recover from mistakes that aren't made in the first place. But best of all is riding perfectly positioned on the wave, fully focused and aware at every moment, aggressively projecting your desire to go forward, riding strongly from one moment comfortably into the next.

As we have seen, mastering riding requires the ability to synchronize several tasks. The rider's body must be balanced and flexible, each leg and hand performing independently and simultaneously to apply the subtlest of pressure to guide the horse. There are any number of sports that can test an athlete's skill and courage, but the mind, body and spirit of the horse makes horsemanship uniquely demanding.

In other sports, if you're not having your best day, it doesn't bother your equipment. Your golf clubs don't care if you slice and your surfboard doesn't care if you fall off. Horses, however, care intensely. Remember, they're counting on us to be the dominant ones, the ones who know what we're doing. So when they sense a wobbly, unbalanced, on-the-edge-of-control rider, it troubles them. It shakes their trust and leads them to rebel against what they are being asked to do. And as we have seen, here's where all sorts of horse behavior problems begin.

So an equestrian must possess more than physical skill. The rider's mind must remain constantly focused on the moment-to-moment application of pressure and weight. The rider must be constantly aware of the surrounding environment, looking for distractions that will shift the horse's focus from the work at hand. The rider's spirit must calmly and confidently project straightforwardness into the horse. We ourselves must possess these skills of the body, mind and spirit so that we can impart to our horses the attributes of impulsion, balance, flexion, focus, awareness, trust, calm, confidence and willingness.

I know. This is a tall order, and that in itself creates another challenge. It's hard to find courage and persistence when being overwhelmed with new information, and it's hard to aim higher when what you're already attempting is dragging you down. "Hard" creates frustration, frustration creates stress, and stress creates resentment, anger and fear. And you know by now that all that will go directly into your horse, making things harder yet. But here's a couple of tips to help you get started.

First, breathe. I know it sounds too simple to be true, but deep, controlled breathing will go a long way toward building the relaxed, focused attitude we need with horses (and in other areas of our lives, too). And breathing's not as simple as you think. Actors and musicians spend hours talking about and working on correct breathing. Meditation starts with deep breaths. Often, our first reaction to stress is to stop breathing or take short, shallow breaths. We can short-circuit this whole feeling if we just stop and focus on a nice, relaxed, in-goes-the-good-air, out-goes-the-bad-air. That will help calm ourselves both on the ground and in the saddle, and our horses will notice. The cornerstone of self-control is breathing.

The second thing to remember is to give yourself a break. You're learning, too. We need to let go of our ego and allow ourselves to make a few mistakes. Impatience is an ego-driven problem. We all want to improve, the sooner the better. Remember: patience. Even a batter in baseball is allowed two strikes before he has to connect. Mistakes are, after all, an essential part of the learning process and people who don't make any mistakes aren't trying anything new.

As well, the riding arena can often feel uncomfortably like a stage, and nobody wants to look bad in public. The trick is to get around that by respecting who we are and where we are at this stage of our development. Think, "I'll get better, but right now this is where I'm at." Competitive athletes cannot reach their peak until they make peace with their desire for recognition. They must stop playing to the crowd and learn to play for the sake of themselves and the sake of the game. If we want to learn patience and respect with our horses, we must first learn it with ourselves.

Let's not, after all, underestimate what we're doing here. We're dealing with powerful forces, and I mean that in the most concrete and physical sense. Controlling the power and strength of a horse and asking more and more difficult and dangerous tasks of it should generate a little stress in the rider. I can tell from personal experience that the stakes in terms of pain and injury are significant. But personal growth doesn't come from avoiding risk, challenge and stress. The key to success is in learning to embrace the stress. If you love your life and where you are and what you're doing, stress is exhilarating and inspiring.

Facing stress and welcoming it under these conditions is the source of optimism, faith, trust and perseverance. If we wait for the stress to end we've missed the point. Stress won't go away; we must make peace with it. We must learn to face these fears just as we ask horses to stop running and face their fear of us.

I think my first inkling of this came back when I was growing up in Swift Current, watching my old girlfriend ride her horse. Like me, she was a bit of a brooding soul with a lot of conflict and doubt in her life. But she was a pretty good rider, and when she was on her horse I could see all that darkness fall away. When I watched her ride, I could see that she was happy.

The ultimate ride on a horse is to take an energy that is calm and ride it as it builds like a gathering storm, swelling with power until the forward wave crescendos to a peak. We surf that peak, riding the balanced, harnessed power. Our lives can be like that too: moving from stasis forward into new challenges and responsibilities, then enjoying the rewards of a new mastery. But of course, it never ends: we get a glimpse of the next level and back we go into the ocean, looking for new surf. Or up we get into the saddle, riding the exhilarating equine wave of mind, body and spirit.

CHAPTER FIVE

TRAINING THE RIDER

At this point, I'm starting to feel like a writer in one of those home decorating magazines. I've described this wonderful room full of grace and beauty that we'd all love to live in. I've told you about how it was designed, all the meaningful objects it contains and how magical the hours spent in there can be. What I haven't told you is how you can enter this room and experience it for yourself. It must be starting to feel as remote a possibility as a perfectly ordered and designed parlor in a household with two kids and a dog.

Well, it needn't be. This room is open to anyone. And while you will still have to walk through them yourself, this chapter will tell you where the doors are. In short, this chapter is about how to effect change — change that will allow you to develop the qualities and skills you need in the horse arena. And maybe in other areas of your life as well.

Change is a journey. Like a journey, it requires preparation. A traveler isn't likely to end up at her desired destination just by setting out and trusting to luck. Before we talk about the path that will lead us to that room we want to be in, we have to pack a little mental luggage.

The first thing in our saddlebag should be a clear, un-equivocal decision that change is needed. If there's one thing that's common to all the self-help books I've read, this is it. Remember our horses' distaste for ambiguity, for weasel words and justifications and rationalizations and excuses? Well, that's the horse showing us how to get started. We have to turn that clear kind of thinking on ourselves. The first question to ask is "Am I satisfied? Am I happy and content?" There's no room for "maybe" or sometimes" or "half-and-half" in our response. Either you want more or you don't. In the same way, you can't answer "I would be happy, if only this or that in my life would change." If you want change, nobody else can do it for you.

This isn't news for most of us and in fact, it's some-thing of a self-help cliché. But that basic insight is just the first step. A clear desire for change is no good without the willpower to drive that change. There's a lot of unused fitness equipment in a lot of basement rec rooms bearing dusty testimony to that. To turn desire into action, we need to believe two things: first, we need to believe that we are worth changing and second, we need to believe that we are capable of change. In short, it's a question of believing in ourselves.

I know, this may not be as easy as I'm making it sound. We all grow up learning attitudes that cling to us like burrs on a saddle blanket. Many people don't even realize that they are living with deep-seated beliefs that hold them back until something shakes them up. My friend Rob, for example, somehow grew up with the idea that he wasn't very athletic. Sure enough, he wasn't. Then he was unemployed for a while. With a lot of time on his hands and not much money to spend, Rob hauled out a pair of old cross-country skis he'd had as a kid, just to fill in his days and work off some frustration. Today, Rob skis marathons and makes tracks all over the mountains. He's got a few bicycle racing trophies, too. Far from thinking himself awkward, and somewhat to his surprise, he's now comfortable and confident in his body.

Chris riding Bahama.

We can't change our height or the color of our eyes, but we can change how we think about ourselves. It takes soul-searching, if for no other reason than to assess what our self-image actually is. It may also take some healing and some letting go of past wrongs. I know from personal experience that most of us have some emotional luggage from our childhood that we're still hauling around. Learn to leave it at the station. You can blame whoever you like for your problems, but that blame is a like a big roadblock keeping you from the confidence you need to move forward. It keeps us from believing in ourselves because it hands over power to someone or something outside ourselves.

Tell yourself to be on guard against blame. Every time you hear yourself blaming your parents or your spouse or your kids or your boss or your employees or your horse, you are in denial. You are denying that you are free to control your own response to the situations life sends you. If you are in the habit of blaming other people and external circumstances for your discontent, then the only way you will be able to go forward effectively is by going back and dealing with your past.

Guilt is another mental habit that sucks the faith and optimism right out of us. It strikes right at the heart of the belief in our own worth that we need to help us change. Lord knows, we all live with some guilt; the trick is to learn to probe into its origin. Are others making us feel guilty because we don't live by their standards? If so, what are our thoughts about those standards? Maybe we need to learn more respect for our own standards. But maybe we're guilty because we're not measuring up to our own standards. Take a minute to ask yourself why not, and write down a few of the answers. If any of them involve blame, see above. Once you know the real roots of that behavior you feel guilty about, ask yourself how you can change that behavior. Here's where your going forward begins.

Now you've packed your bags with the right attitudes. It's time to think about the journey, time to draw a few maps. You can't ride a horse without telling it where to go, and you can't engineer change in yourself without setting some goals. There's a common theme in the self-help movement that dates all the way back to Dale Carnegie winning friends and influencing people, and that's the power of positive thinking. We have to be cautious with this attitude. We're told over and over that we can do anything if we psyche ourselves up enough, even walk on fire, as if the human mind were as simple as the Little Engine That Could saying "I think I can, I think I can."

Positive thinking is fine, but unless you've already given a lot of serious thought about what you want to achieve, you're just huffing and puffing. You can't brainwash yourself into success without first knowing exactly what it is you're aiming for. All that energy spent striving for improvement with your horse or happiness in your life is going to be wasted if you don't know where you're going.

This is a tricky one. Everyone's going to find their own goals differently. And what's more, it's not something you do once and then never have to do again. Goals change over the course of our lives, sometimes radically. For that reason, it's often just as important to know how to find what's important to us as it is to have the answer. The process can be just as important as the result.

For me, it began with learning to listen to my subconscious rather than trying to program it. Dreams at night told me much about who I was and what I wanted. I found it useful to write them down in a little note-pad I kept by my bed. I learned it was important to write down whatever was in my head, whether or not it was pleasant for me or someone I cared about. And then I gave myself time to think about what I had written.

Lists are another useful tool for goal-setting. Just like when you're shopping for groceries, lists can help us organize our thinking and make sure we cover all the bases. Make lists of everything you want to change about yourself, physically, mentally and spiritually. Lay them out in front of you and compare them. Do they reinforce or contradict each other? For example, are you asking your spirit to be more spontaneous and your mind to think things through more carefully? Then, make another list of what is keeping you from making these changes. Think about the roots of these roadblocks. Do they originate from within yourself, in feelings of blame or guilt? Ask yourself what you need to do to overcome them.

Once you've got a reasonably clear idea of your goals, decide which ones are the most important. Write them down. I find writing them down makes them seem more attainable. Remember to break big, long-term goals down into manageable steps. For example, if you make $30,000 a year and your goal is to make $100,000 annually, you are setting yourself up for failure unless you understand that before 30 becomes 100 it must first become 31, then 32, and then 33. If your horse improves one per cent a week, within two years he'll be 100 per cent better.

All packed with a reasonably reliable map of your destination, carrying a load of the right mental baggage, you should be ready for your journey of change. But before you set off, here's a few travel tips that I've found useful, some mental and physical exercises that will help you keep moving forward.

Learn to breathe. Nothing is more important to your body than breathing, yet it is the first thing to be thrown out of whack when we are stressed. Many unproductive mental states are linked to similar physical states — tension, for example. And you can't approach a horse, or anything else, with a calm, confident, loose manner if your head is all ajangle with fear and confusion. Controlled, regular breathing can help a lot. Think of a woman giving birth: to keep herself as calm and strong as she can, she focuses on breathing. Faced with a tough situation, learn to take a second to remind yourself to inhale and exhale deeply, completely and regularly. Practise this so you can do it easily when you need to.

Feel your body. We communicate with our horses mostly through our body, so we need to be as fluent with it as we can. Get in shape. Use your body. Develop a physical program that focuses on flexibility, not just strength. Disciplines such as yoga or Tai Chi or other martial arts courses are very suitable for this. A simple routine of stretching before your regular riding session or whatever sport you do can go a long way.

Nurture your spirit. I believe meditation is the basis of all spiritual discipline. Meditation is not the absence of thought; it's allowing the mind to let its thoughts flow unrestricted and unjudged. Give your mind the unedited freedom to allow your spirit to come to the surface of your thoughts. Soon, with practice, your spirit will come to life and give you inspiration and guidance. And this will be a powerful source of optimism are fortitude to face the challenges of change.

Repeat affirmations. In practice, our mind is rarely still and quiet. It always seems to need a bone to chew on. However, we can decide what that bone will be. When doing a job that doesn't require your full attention — doing the dishes, weeding the garden — try using the opportunity to program your mind. Find yourself a mantra that furthers your goals: "I am relaxed and centered," or "I am free of guilt," or "I ride tall in the saddle." Soon enough, these little affirmations will take on a life of their own and you'll hear yourself saying them when you need them the most.

Visualize success. This is a very common and powerful tool used by athletes in training. When you're having trouble accomplishing a particular maneuver or feat, sit quietly and run a movie in your mind of successfully completing the task. Imagine exactly what you want to do, then close your eyes and run the film over and over. Run it in slow motion and carefully savor the details of your performance. You will find this much easier and more effective if you've already learned to clear and calm your mind through breathing and meditation.

Reject judgment. When you get something wrong, resist the temptation to see it as a reflection of your own worth. Don't think "I can't get my horse to turn left around that obstacle. I'm such a loser." Instead, use your visualization skills to examine what you're doing objectively. Don't assign labels of wrong or right; just try and analyze what you're doing and where your body is at each step. Instead of looking for things you're doing wrong, look for ways to make what you're doing work better. Nobody gets everything right the first time. The sooner you realize that, the sooner you'll be able to learn from your mistakes instead of letting them defeat you.

Recognize success. When something works for you, take a moment to savor it. Use your visualization skills to replay it in your mind. Try to remember how it felt in your body. Draw on those memories when you have to repeat the act, remembering that no two situations are ever exactly the same.

Don't forget to laugh. Keep things in perspective. Remember to have fun. Obviously, none of these suggestions are going to teach how to saddle your horse, jump a fence or perform a flying lead change. Those are technical skills and teaching them is not my intent in this chapter.

The point I do want to make is that following these guidelines is going to make learning those specific technical skills a lot easier. Furthermore, horses will respond much better to a rider who learns to cultivate a calm, collected mind and spirit, untroubled by self-defeating emotions. And in my experience, so will people.

All through this book, I've stressed the importance of a clear, confident stance toward your horse, an attitude that doesn't have to be put on like a pair of riding boots because it comes naturally from within. I know, developing this attitude is a lot harder than I make it sound in a series of neat paragraphs. It will take time. It will take work. Just remember that change is inevitable, so we might as well work toward change for the better. Ask yourself every day "Did I move a little forward toward my goal today?" If the answer is yes, then there's a law of physics that's working in our favor: an object in motion tends to remain in motion. If we are patient and focused, improvement, like bank interest, will compound.

CHAPTER SIX

CHARACTER AND CONSCIOUSNESS

We've been pretty physical so far in this book. We've watched horses in the field, we've worked with them on the ground and finally, we've mounted them and begun riding. We've talked a bit about the attitudes necessary to approach this work, but now it's time to let our thoughts whirl a bit further out and think about some of the wider consequences of this kind of horsemanship.

At the end of the first chapter, I was standing in the middle of a round pen, horses swirling around me. At that point, I was slowly becoming a teacher and starting to think more deeply about what I was doing. I was cataloguing all the things I'd learned — or tried to learn — since I started working with horses and was looking ahead to the new directions my ideas were taking. I'd like now to return to that figure surrounded by pounding hooves and roiling dust. The previous chapters have detailed what he's learned about the demands horses place on his body and his mind. What about his spirit?

Most of what I had learned to that point was the result of instinct, repetition, painful experience and bonehead luck. Not a course of study I would recommend — it takes a long time and leaves a lot of bruises. But it was the only one I knew and it worked for me, even if it did leave me operating on the level of intuition and what felt right. It was my wife Anita's perceptive and persistent questioning that forced me to think out loud and articulate what I was doing and why it worked. The last several chapters are the result of what she started. But once this process of self-examination began, it picked up a momentum of its own. And as I probed into what I was doing with the horse, I also started to think about what the horse was doing with me. Two things were changing: my character and my consciousness.

I've already hinted at some of the qualities that working with horses will call up in you, if you let it happen. Mostly, those discussions have come as an afterthought, as we were chiefly concerned with the horse. Now it's time to turn our gaze inward and examine those qualities a little more closely. We've talked a lot about confidence, and with good reason. If respect is the most important feeling a horse can have toward us, confidence is the most important feeling we must develop toward the horse. As we've seen, respect and confidence are the proper roots of the horse/trainer relationship. Nothing gets accomplished without them and unless they're firmly established, all kinds of behavior problems creep in.

We know that respect means focus, trust and control. So what do we mean by confidence? Well, confidence is not is a cocksure swagger, a booming voice and a heavy hand. That's not confidence, it's bluster, and it's worse than useless in the horse arena — and anywhere else, for that matter. For us, confidence has more to do with knowing exactly what we want, being resolute about achieving it, and expressing that knowledge and resolution in everything we say and do.

Think of a major-league batter stepping up to the plate. He doesn't come in talking trash to the pitcher or pointing to where in the stands he's going to smash the ball (unless he's Babe Ruth). He steps up firmly, grips the bat, settles into his stance and coolly looks out toward the mound. At that moment everything in his mind and his body is saying: "I will hit this ball." Of course, chances are he'll go down on strikes, pop out or get tagged at first base. Even a good hitter only gets on base once in every three at-bats. The batter knows that too, but he doesn't let that dent his inner surety. And every now and then, he'll knock one out of the park.

This is the kind of confidence I came to understand that horses needed from me. Because it has purged itself of conflicting desires and knows clearly what it wants, this confidence is calm and still. Because it is reflected in every word and gesture, it's consistent. Because it understands that there will be setbacks, it doesn't get easily rattled. Because it reflects the mind's desires clearly through the body, it's transparent.

Horses respond to this kind of confidence, and it comes into play both in the round pen and in the saddle. It doesn't take much to make a horse nervous, maybe only an unfamiliar object like a new garbage can alongside a familiar path. When a horse does come up to something that upsets it, the first thing it does is ask its rider "How do we feel about this?" The worst thing that rider can do is feed the horse's apprehension. A tuned-in rider will know to look for the question and then be able to clearly respond "I don't have a problem with it. It's OK." Relieved, the horse will carry on.

Confidence is closely related to the next quality that horsemanship will draw out in a person. Once you're clear about what you want and are confidently expressing it, you are able to focus. We've already talked about the need for focus. Focus doesn't mean narrowing down your attention to a few details of horse behavior. It means paying attention to and balancing a wide variety of inputs. While our body is engaged in the moment-to-moment task of pushing the horse forward, our mind must also be totally aware of the constant messages being sent back from the horse. Our mind must be focused on responding immediately to those messages or even anticipating them with the appropriate measure of forward pressure.

Meanwhile, our spirit must project a continuous aura of calm determination to be the leader of this dance between human and horse. We have to be able to do all this at the same time. Compare two camera lenses: while the telephoto lens isolates small details of a scene, we need to be the wide-angle lens that sees the big picture and brings everything into equally sharp relief.

We also need to be able keep this lens in focus over the long haul. Like our horses, we are easily distracted and too often, we come to the ring with a head full of unrelated thoughts and issues and general mental noise. But if we want our horses to learn to focus their attention on us, we must learn to focus ours on them. That's easy enough to do in spurts. The real trick is to learn to maintain it for as long as we need to. There's no automatic pilot on horses. They're constantly sending you messages and they constantly need some response. Horses, by being so sensitive to our self-doubts and fears, allow us to spot them in ourselves and root them out.

As our confidence grows and our ability to focus increases, we need to learn how to use strength to put our desires into play. Strength can be a tricky one. Make no mistake, we need it. We're trying to dominate an animal much bigger than ourselves that has definite ideas of its own. It's going to get physical out there. The only question is how much strength, and when.

Men tend to rely too much on strength — and not just in the horse ring. Plenty of home handymen, confronted with a part that doesn't quite slide into place, growl "I'll make it fit." Then they reach for the hammer, or as it's called in these situations, The Persuader. Often as not, they break the part and have to start over. Horses don't respond well to that type of persuasion any better than hardware does. Nor do many other situations, really.

Women, on the other hand, are sometimes afraid to use a little muscle. They're brought up to believe that just a little more love and nurturing will solve any problem. This, unfortunately, isn't always the case — especially with a herd animal like a horse which needs to know where it fits in the hierarchy of the herd.

The challenge is to dominate and lead without abusing. Too little force and you won't realize your goals in anything. Your horse won't do what you ask, your children will walk all over you and your employees won't follow your agenda. Too much force, and all of the above will respond with fear, not respect, and will eventually rebel against you. Judgment is the key. Clear, confident goals and accurate, focused understanding give us the tools we need to develop and use our strength with good judgment. A real Mr. Fixit soon learns that considering the problem, then sliding the stubborn part home with just the right twist works a lot better than bashing it with a mallet.

But judgment must also be tempered by two other qualities: empathy and patience. We can't only take our own goals and understanding into account when we're trying to respond to behavior. It's vital to understand where the other side is coming from on both rational and emotional levels. This empathy will give us much greater insight into what we're really asking and how far we expect the horse to come. Once we understand and act on that insight, patience comes naturally.

Often, we're not aware of how hard what we're asking really is. A friend of mine once explained how that lesson was brought home to him. Gerry was training to be a life-guard and swimming instructor. He was, of course, an excellent swimmer and completely at home in the pool. Diving off the board was no big deal. So to make him understand how scary the diving board was for a kid in his first or second year of lessons, Gerry's instructors took him up the high board, blindfolded him, and told him to jump. "That's what your kids feel like when you ask them to jump off the regular board," they said. With that lesson firmly in mind, Gerry went on to become a fine swim teacher.

The next quality that grows from true horsemanship flows from these lessons of patience and turning toward the other's point of view. Horse people — all people, I believe — should learn humility. Our egos would have us think that we are always right the first time and that to admit error is to be diminished. When we're wrong in public — and nothing can feel more public than a riding arena — we lose face. No one wants to lose any of those things, and this is how our egos hold us back and keep us from venturing outside what we already know. Humility can set us free from those ego-imposed re-straints by allowing us to acknowledge our ignorance. Humility gives us permission to be wrong; it shows us the length of our own journey and allows us to grasp that it's going to take a bit of traveling. Humility al-lows us to stop worrying about how others see us and lets us focus on where we actually are. It makes patience with ourselves possible.

There's something I call the law of 1-2-3-4; it's my
way of describing the learning curve of both humans and
horses. Say you're trying to get a horse to do something,
maybe to go all the way into a corner instead of shying
away. You work at it and work at it, and eventually the
horse does what you want. But that's just once. Once is

PHOTO: JIM KNELSON

luck. You keep at it, and the horse does it right the next time, too. But that's just twice. Twice is coincidence. The next time around, the horse gets it right again. That's three — the horse has spotted a pattern. If the horse does it right the fourth time in a row, then he's learned something.

People often learn in the same way, not only in simple physical skills but in complex matters central to our lives. Few of us find real love without going through three or four serious relationships first. It's almost as common to find someone who's experienced several different fields before settling into their true career. We have to accept these false starts and not think less of ourselves because of them. Humility lets us do that. It allows us to reclaim our past by showing that it wasn't just a series of mistakes, it was the path we took to get where we are. In the same way, acknowledging we'll probably mess up again makes it easier for us to try something new. Humility frees us to explore our future path.

And once humility has removed the roadblock of ego, horsemanship will now call up one final quality - courage. Not just physical courage — although you'll need that, too — but the courage to change. Just as our horses need to go forward, we also need to find the courage to take risks and go forward as well. We need courage to accept the danger we face with horses and the courage to accept the mantle of leadership we ask them to grant us. These kinds of courage are often the hardest to find. But with our calm, focused confidence, patient strength and humble awareness of our ignorance, we're already well on the way.

But horsemanship can change more than just character. The more time I spent with horses and the more I thought about things, the more I came to realize that my new, emerging understanding of myself was only half the story. For me, the final step in my journey came when I realized the impact horses were having on the way I understood the world.

For example, I've already talked a little bit about what I've called prey consciousness: an orientation toward overall awareness instead of narrow, focused concentration on a goal. To recap briefly, humans are hunters, and hunters learn to concentrate their attention on their prey. A moment's distraction can cost the kill and endanger the survival of the pack. It's effective — humans, after all, are a pretty successful species — but it tends to reduce the world to two categories: food or not-food, and everything not-food can be safely ignored. Horses, however, are prey. Their food — grass — is all around them, so there's no need to focus on the particular patch they're grazing on. Their survival depends on detecting and warding off attacks from hunters, and for that they have learned to be highly attuned to everything in their environment. A predator is interested in the grazing deer; prey are interested in the entire meadow.

And that is one of the most valuable things horses have to teach us. Sure, like Joshu, we can learn poise and balance, to walk on the balls of our feet and stay alert to our surroundings. That's worth knowing, but there's more here than that. What we really need to learn is that the world is more than a gallery of prey — and I use that word in the broadest sense. Sometimes our prey is money, sometimes it's power, sometimes it's sex or success. Whatever we're stalking, we have to realize that there's more to the world than a place for us to conduct our hunts, thinking only of our own ends with no concern for the context of our actions.

Like a herd of horses, we must become sensitive to the interactions and interrelationships between ourselves and the people and world around us. Also like a herd of horses, we must come to realize that our survival depends on those linkages and cross-fertilizations. To behave otherwise is destructive both socially and environmentally, and there's just too little of the natural world left for us to keep hunting down and killing whatever of it we desire.

We'll always remain predators and we'll always need something to hunt. But if we learn to think more like prey, we'll get better at putting the results of that hunt in context. Maybe we'd find new goals to chase down and conquer, goals that strengthen rather than weaken the social and natural fabric of our world. Horses don't only show us what we must learn; they show us how to use that knowledge.

Think back to our discussion on how horses compete. They compete with each other while keeping the welfare of the herd in mind. Horses know they have to stick together to survive, so the loser of a battle for dominance is not vanquished. In a way, the loser is strengthened because he now has an ally more powerful than himself to rely on. The herd is also strengthened, as the chain of authority is clarified and those most fit to lead rise to the top without the loss of any members. It's competition, serious competition, but it's non-destructive.

Pondering all this set me up for the last and deepest lesson I believe horses have to teach us. Remember our discussion about dualism or, more accurately, polarity? Earlier, I described the type of qualities that being a predator summon up in us. Boldness, confidence, courage, strength. Humans love a challenge, undertake quests and focus on goals. We see the world as a stage for individual action.

But then I went on to say that we have much to learn from prey consciousness. And prey consciousness is all about observing, not acting; receiving and understanding the world as it is, not going out and changing it. Prey consciousness sees unities instead of parts and makes connections instead of breaks. Individuals take their meaning and worth from their role in the group.

We see this polarity again and again. Some call it the struggle between passion and reason; others, instinct versus intellect. It opens up every time we have to decide whether to follow our head or our heart. It colors our idea of the human journey: we associate youth with passion and inspiration, while maturity is thought of as cooler and more calculating. It also shapes how we look at the world, for the natural world is considered free and spontaneous while civilization is called artificial and rule-bound. And although both sexes share qualities on either side of this divide, this polarity continues to be the greatest influence on how we think about gender.

The greatest lesson horses have to teach us is how to resolve this polarity and bring together these two sides of our nature. If we can think like predators and feel like prey, as I believe horses want us to, I am convinced that would go a long way toward healing our wounds within. We would live easier with each other, and yet we could retain and nurture the spark and crackle that makes the human adventure worth experiencing.

Ultimately, I don't think we can confront our deepest attitudes toward ourselves and our world without looking toward the Power that lies behind them. I believe that just as we must teach our horses to conquer their fear, stop running and focus their attention on us, we must also learn to face our fears and stop running from God.

Humans fear spirit just as horses fear us because we believe that nurturing our spirit will force us to sacrifice. We won't be able to do as we please any longer, we will lose our freedom, we may even die. But just as a horse can find freedom and trust in its relationship with its rider, we can find the same things in our relationship with, well, call it The Creator, call it Jehovah, call it the Great Spirit, or even call it Fred if you like.

We are here to allow our spirit to drive our body and our mind forward in the experience of life. We are to learn to be responsive to the constant flow of experience that life has to offer us and to direct and control that flow to find our goals. As we focus on the spirit, we discover a realm of balance and harmony. Just as our work in the round pen is a dance, life is a dance too, sometimes frantic, sometimes a slow waltz. But we are always meant to face the spirit and ask it where we should go. And the answer will come back: "Forward."

CHAPTER SEVEN

ETIQUETTE

This story has come a long way, from Swift Current to Seattle to Nevada, and the inner journey has been even longer. But there's still a little way left to go and one more lesson for you and I to learn. To complete the circle, I need to pick up the threads I put down a few chapters ago. I need to talk about the horse that taught me you *can* go home again.

I left off telling my story when I was still in Nevada. It was 1993 and I was doing pretty well training, buying and selling horses. Some of my horses, especially the Mustangs I worked with, were winning state and national championships. I was the young up-and-comer, a growing fish in a good-sized regional pond.

Through my wife Anita, who was a riding instructor at a large local equestrian center, I had been introduced to the world of English riding and was beginning to make inroads into that community. In fact, the owner of the place where Anita worked — the Carson Valley Equestrian Center — invited me to move in and become the resident trainer.

It was while training horses at that facility that I first heard of Willy Arts, a Dutch dressage trainer and well-known breeder who lives in Fresno, California. That's where he raised and trained Olympic-class dressage horses. Willy used to come through our place once a month for a clinic and he was coaching at one of these events when he noticed somebody driving horses in the next arena. Impressed at the driver's skill, he grew more and more distracted until he finally asked the crowd if anyone knew who that guy over there was. Luckily, Anita was in the audience and she spoke up: "That's my husband." So Willy and I got together and we hit it off. Willy liked how I handled a team and he liked how I handled unruly horses. And, as it happened at the time, Willy had an unruly horse that needed a lot of handling.

This horse was something to see. First off, he was huge — a big old warmblood 16.2 hands high, tall enough to stand shoulder to shoulder with me with his head towering over me. And I'm not short. He was also handsome, strong and big-boned, and had an amazing amount of what horse folk call presence — a tough thing to define, but it's the same quality that in people marks a born leader or draws your eye inevitably towards a movie star.

But this was one troubled animal. He was mean, angry, and very nasty. He attacked both people and other horses with equal fury. He'd chase grooms out of his stable and they couldn't even walk other horses by him. He was no bluff, just really bad. His name, ironically enough, was Etiquette.

Etiquette had been brought to California by a woman who dreamed of starting her own high-end breeding farm.

He was of the finest, purest pedigree and a couple of his brothers were on European Olympic equestrian teams. Etiquette was intended to be the foundation sire of an entire breeding program. But those kind of dreams don't come cheap and the woman who was chasing them ran into money problems.

Etiquette's training was delayed again and again. Despite his value, this magnificent animal's development was neglected. Eventually, Etiquette's owner went out of business and ultimately, his training never even started. The woman owed Willy money and in lieu of some of that cash, he took over Etiquette.

By this time, Etiquette was five or six years old. Believe it or not, he'd never been ridden. He'd never even been started. He'd been left a stallion — although Willy was soon to change that — but he'd never covered a mare. You couldn't even put a halter on him and grooms had to feed him by throwing hay over the fence at him. Then they put water in his trough while Etiquette was distracted by the food. He was that mean. "He'll never make a woman's horse," Willy said. And because the great majority of dressage riders are women, he decided to turn Etiquette into a driving horse.

That's when he asked me to see what I could do with him. Train this beast to the point where he's saleable and we can split the money 50-50, Willy said. Again, I agreed. But I almost wished I hadn't when Willy drove out to our place to deliver Etiquette. There he was, rearing up in the air, screaming and hollering, the snarliest and angriest horse I'd ever seen. I swallowed hard when I realized this was my project.

We let him sit in his stall at Carson Valley for a day. The next day, with 30 or 40 people watching, I stepped into the pen with him for his first session. Sure enough, Etiquette came at me. I was more like a rodeo clown than a trainer for a while as I dodged his attacks. But I didn't let that huge horse chase me out of the pen and I didn't give up. I kept right on playing horse with him, challenging and trying to dominate him in the same way I'd done hundreds of times before and the same way I've described earlier in this book.

And Etiquette tried to do the same with me. We were running circles around the pen, sometimes Etiquette chasing me and sometimes me chasing Etiquette. It was loud, aggressive body language all right. For 45 minutes, we shouted at each other with our gestures and pushed into each other's space as we fought over who was going to be the boss. Eventually, it was me. After a long hour had passed, Etiquette finally submitted. And when he did, he came all the way. Focused and centered, he walked right up in front of me. It was beautiful.

I could see his anger beginning to give way to a serious work ethic, so I kept at him. I haltered him and gave him his first lesson on a lunge line. I didn't stop there, either. I kept working my way in closer and closer from the lunging position of about 20-25 feet out. Closer and closer I got, until I was almost driving him from the side.

I improvised a set of reins out of the halter rope. And then I just swung up on the back of this big, scary horse and he let me do it. He was a little outraged at my presumption, but he let me do it.

Right away, I felt a powerful connection with this horse. I felt as if we were somehow each other's destiny. I turned him left and I turned him right, and when I squeezed him up into a trot it was the biggest wave I'd ever felt in my life. It was like going from bobbing around on a lake to surfing Hawaii.

By the end of the first week, we were riding cross-country, jumping bushes and crossing creeks. And he still had that presence, that powerful male energy. When Etiquette and I came trotting along, other horses and riders just parted before us. I knew I couldn't sell him at this point and I bought him outright from Willy. With Etiquette underneath me, Willy was able to teach me all kinds of things about dressage I wouldn't have been able to learn on any lesser horse.

Anita rode him too, introducing him to show jumping. She sometimes allowed the best of her students to ride him, just to feel what that kind of energy was like. After our work with Etiquette, Willy once announced to a group of his peers "When you've got a good horse, call me. When you've got a bad horse, call Chris." That felt pretty good. And sure, I'm proud of what we were able to accomplish with Etiquette. But that's not why he's such an important part of this story.

With all the other horses I've trained, their spirit became a tiny bit smaller after I was finished with them, their energy slightly dimmed. The change grew less noticeable as I got better at my work, but something was

Recent photo of Etiquette at a show in California.

always lost in the domination. And I never felt I was achieving complete unity with a horse if I was asking it to give something up that I didn't have to. Etiquette, however, lost nothing. He had submitted to me with complete trust, but it didn't cost him one iota of his presence, his energy, his equine machismo. Riding Etiquette convinced me that the balance I've been talking about isn't just an ideal or a pretty piece of New Age theory. It's as real as flexing muscle and flying mane. Etiquette was living, galloping proof it is possible to balance both the cooperative and competitive sides of our nature and compromise neither of them.

And one more thing. Kept isolated from both horses and humans, nobody had ever played horse with Etiquette. That's a terribly unnatural situation for a horse. But it turned out that what this "bad" horse wanted most of all was to join up with someone. He just needed to be challenged on his terms, in a language he could understand. Once he had been, and was convinced to face and put aside his fear and anger, he was the greatest horse I've ever ridden.

Etiquette's willingness to go beyond his painful history and move on to accept the work he had been born to do made a deep impression on me. I guess I was susceptible about then, because things were coming together for our little family. Anita and I had a daughter by now, our beautiful little Raven, and we wanted to raise her in our native country. We also felt there would be a lot of opportunity for our kind of work in Canada. And truth to tell, we were starting to feel a little homesick. So as I watched Etiquette transcend the trauma of his past, I came to realize that I too had made a lot of progress dealing with my own childhood and that maybe it was time for me to stop running away from things. It was time to come home. That's what we decided to do.

There was, however, a catch. We knew we would need some start-up money. We looked around for options, but we both understood that Etiquette was our greatest asset. To return to Canada, we would have to sell the horse who helped us realize it was time to go. We started looking for a buyer who would give him the home he deserved and eventually, we sold him to a woman who belonged to a hunt club in Nevada and needed a big, strong, spirited horse to chase coyotes over hills and through creeks and over bushes. That's where Etiquette went, to ride pell-mell through the desert countryside. I thought he'd like that, but it didn't make the transaction any easier for me. I'd bought and sold hundreds of horses by that time, some pretty good ones too, but that was the only time I really felt a twang in my heart when one of my animals walked into somebody else's trailer. I've always been able to let them go, but losing Etiquette was hard.

It was, however, the money from Etiquette's sale that gave us enough capital to make our new start. So in 1995, we moved to Stewart Valley, Saskatchewan, not 30 miles from my old Swift Current stomping grounds. How's that for coming full circle? Now I'm back in my prairie roots, raising our family amid the wooded coulees and short-grass prairie along the South Saskatchewan River. From our ranch, I travel out to share what I've learned and at home, I work with horses to give them a new start.

Raven and my little boy Adler often watch me when I'm working horses around the ranch, and that's one of my greatest pleasures. But as they watch me in our round pen, the center of a pounding ring of horses, they have no idea how those circling animals have inspired my thoughts to spiral out over the years. Lord knows I had no idea where they were going to take me, either.

And sometimes, when I consider that I'll have enough to do for the rest of my life just working through what my horses have already shown me, it feels like that journey is over. The challenge now is to stay on the path I've started and to practise the life that I'm preaching. I don't feel so much these days like I'm reacting to my past. Thank God, I think I'm finally through with the bad old days and, like my horses, I'm moving forward.

But I know my journey isn't really over. There's always more to learn and what feels like a destination is probably just a new beginning, the next rotation of the circle. And always, horses stomp and whirl around me, my thoughts astride them, riding forward into new and deeper understanding.

EPILOGUE

I began this book with a promise of magic. As we've gone along I've done my best to describe the magic of horses and how to find it, for magic is exactly what horses have been in my life. I believe that magic is available to us all, and most of us, in our desire for transformation and growth, can use all the magic we can get. But still, it seems like a lot to ask of an animal, no matter how strong and beautiful. Haven't horses got enough to carry without filling their saddlebags full of our dreams and needs?

The answer is that horses have been carrying that load for us for as long as we've been together. The spiritual relationship that exists between horses and humans is ancient and well-documented and is no New Age fad. Neither are stories of those who have understood that relationship.

Belief in the magical power of horses was widespread in the ancient world. Horses were used as clan totems as far back as the early Stone Age, when they also came to symbolize the cosmic order of the universe. By the time of the ancient Greeks, horses were keeping company with the Gods, especially those Gods associated with the sun and with water. But at around the same time, the tribes of northern Europe were going one better.

Chris long lining a two-year-old Morgan gelding.

To these people, the horses themselves were godlike. The ancient Celts were a nomadic people to whom the horse was essential equipment. They needed horses to move, to help them fight their enemies and to establish social prestige. Perhaps that's why they had such a well-developed idea of the divine horse. Epona was her name — she was generally represented as a mare or a woman on horseback — and she was associated with freedom and creativity, as well as with fertility and battle.

The name Epona seems to have appeared first among Celtic tribes in Gaul during the Roman Empire and her worship soon spread throughout northern Europe. In fact, the Roman cavalry legions occupying these areas adopted

Epona for themselves, honoring her under the name Epona Augustus or Epona Regina. Under the names Rhiannon and Macha, she also had devotees in what is now Wales and Ireland. Her shrines were common in stables and barns, and some people think that the pre-Christian horse effigies in England are ancient sites dedicated to Epona. Carved into a chalky hillside in Berkshire, England, is the graceful, stylized image known as the White Horse of Uffington. It is believed to be a representation of Epona from the first century AD.

Just as these ancient cultures recognized the spiritual power of horses, they also recognized the spiritual bond between horse and rider. Leaders in the old Teutonic clans swore oaths by the heads of their riding horses. If those promises were broken, the heads of both were severed. The link was even more explicit in the tale of the Irish mythical hero Cu Chulain, who could live no longer than his horses.

Tales of people who understood these bonds and used them to communicate with horses are just as old. The Roman historian Tacitus wrote of a group of Germanic priests who cared for some sacred horses and used their snorts to tell the future. Stories of men who used charms, herbs, or magic words to tame unwilling horses are common throughout Britain and date back to at least the sixth century AD. There was probably more to their technique than that, but it is true that these old-time horse whisperers existed. They even had a union. The Horseman's Word was a secretive, hard-to-crack guild that preserved their secrets of horse management as well as a good working knowledge of horse medicine.

Some of these traditional horsemen are known to us by name. In late 1700s, an Irishman named Sullivan became famous for quieting unruly horses, which he claimed to do by whispering an Indian word in their ear. As one account said, "He would lead the animals away into a darkened barn and no one knew for sure what happened when he closed the door ... All the witnesses knew, was that when Sullivan led the horses out again, all fury had vanished."

In those days, such an ability created a certain amount of public awe and fear. In 1760, a mysterious man named Benjamin Gold became friendly with King Louis XV of France because of his skill quieting horses. Eventually, however, he was accused of dabbling in the occult. A successful demonstration of his skill before all the court didn't help — Gold was forced to flee to England, and eventually, they say, to the court of Catherine the Great in Russia.

I'm not suggesting that we should all become neo-pagans and build shrines to Epona. Nor do I think we should accept those old horse whispering stories as gospel, either. I'm just pointing out that I'm not the first person to come to these conclusions about the spiritual power of the horse and its relationship to us. People have been bringing this power into their lives for thousands of years. There are many historical precedents for what I'm saying. There's a thread here, a thread of magic, and I believe it's no coincidence that people are starting to pick it up again.

As Western civilization progressed, we became so pre-occupied with the practical uses of our horses that the spiritual side of our relationship has been overshadowed. It's not hard to see why, given the importance of the horse to our development. Their strength tilled our farmland and carried our goods. Their courage took us to war. Right up until the Industrial Revolution, the fastest way to get anywhere on land was on horseback. They have been so important to the daily business of human life that horse ownership was the best measure of someone's wealth and power. Any job that required power or speed required horses, and Western civilization would be hard to imagine without them.

Now, of course, those days are gone. Our farms are mechanized and our cavalry divisions drive tanks. We fly quickly and easily from place to place through skies that once belonged to Pegasus. Except in a few specialized cases, horses no longer serve any practical purpose. For the first time in human history, we have no need of the horse's physical strength. What we do need, perhaps more than ever, is the horse's spiritual power. We need that power to resolve conflicts within ourselves and between ourselves. We need that power to bring us back together with our damaged planet. Great as the horse's gifts to us have already been, this one may be the greatest.

Today, the human spirit is poised for transformation. That old predatorial warrior spirit has brought us a long way, but it is now struggling to achieve a balance with the peaceful co-existence of prey consciousness. Many women are well on the way to that balance. Men, always waiting to the last minute, are beginning to consciously search for their own path to a greater sense of spiritual identity. It is imperative that people stop attacking themselves, each other, and the earth and learn relationships that are mutually advantageous. Win-lose is predator thinking. We see now a new age of horse people that are committed to making peace with nature — the hardest lesson that western culture has to learn. But we'll learn it. We have to.

As for me, I still think a lot about Etiquette. I mentioned the powerful, almost predestined connection I felt with that horse — believe me, I've been on a lot of horses and I've never felt anything like that before. It was as if he was the horse that would allow me to realize my ideals and, in fact, that's what he turned out to be.

A horse like that you want to ride for the rest of your life. I've had close relationships with quite a few horses, but with Etiquette I wanted to develop that bond for years and years and see how deep we could get. It didn't work out that way. But I haven't given up hope. If there is a next cycle for me, it will begin when I find another horse to ride along that path that Etiquette and I began. This horse I'll buy and train as carefully as I can. And I'll never sell him.

I can see him in my dreams — or rather, I can see both of us. We're doing the kind of riding I've always loved best, roaming free over the prairie, down into willowed coulees and up over the silver-saged benchlands. Sometimes we're at full gallop, sometimes an ambling walk, sometimes I'm just dozing on the grass in the sun while my horse grazes idly nearby. And in that dream, I can feel us talk. Just whispers really — a few words, a snort, a gesture, a flicked tail is all we'll need to know exactly what the other is thinking and feeling. To others, it'll look like magic. And you know what? They'll be right.

AFTERWORD

Three years have passed since I wrote those dreaming words about how I hoped I would soon be able to laze around in the shortgrass while my new horse grazed nearby. And in those three years, many of the dreams I had expressed have indeed come true — although not exactly in the way I expected. Just when you think you've got things all mapped out, life has a way of surprising you. As I'd sensed, I was about to enter a new cycle of exploring the horse-human polarity. But I thought I was about to mount the back of a second horse like Etiquette and see how complete a unity we could achieve. I thought I was about to get closer to the horse side of the equation. Instead, I was about to get closer to the people side. Just as I'd hoped when our little family moved back home to Saskatchewan, it turned out there was indeed an audience for what I had to show and say. I was mostly training horses at home and also going out on the road about 50 days per year to give clinics.

After this book was first published, I began to tour more seriously, conducting clinics at first across Canada and then into the United States. I soon found myself on the road 200 days a year and as you might imagine, that was a real emotional challenge for my family. I'll never repay the debt of gratitude I owe Anita for keeping our home more than just together, but genuinely happy. I spoke at quite a few horse conventions and met many other renowned trainers. I learned from almost all of them, even though most of us thought quite a bit alike. I watched lots of round pen work and I met lots of trainers with a pretty good understanding of how the mind of a horse thinks. But as I conducted workshops in little towns and big arenas all across the continent, I was starting to notice something that no one else, I thought, had picked out.

At clinic after clinic, something was beginning to happen that I had only sensed before. This didn't happen all the time, but people kept coming up to me after a demonstration and would say something like: "This is amazing. You walked out there and talked about horses for two hours and all I could think about was how it applied to everything else in my life." When I began giving clinics, I had been afraid that my thoughts and ideas were just too far out there — that I had ventured far beyond what most people were even prepared to think about, let alone accept. I felt I was taking a big risk. The last thing I needed was to end up labelled as some kind of New Age flake by the conservative and often close-minded horse industry. But as it turned out, I needn't have worried. I wasn't that far ahead at all and many people were ready to listen. They were making similar connections all on their own. It got so I could predict when the penny would drop. I knew, for example, when I was talking about giving respect to get it and controlling behaviour through indirect pressure, some woman in the audience would ask jokingly but hopefully: "Does it work on husbands?" Someone asked that question at every clinic I gave. Every single one.

Sensing the interest, I responded. I still did plenty of lectures and demonstrations of round pen work, but I began to broaden the metaphors I used. I talked about how, when we're riding, our mind should be like the captain of a sailboat because the mind of the horse is very much like the wind. Everybody inherently knows that a sailor does not fight with or make vain attempts to control the wind by force but instead learns to become accountable for how well he or she can work with their sails. I began to talk about the relationship between the dance in the round pen and the rest of our lives. And as I did more of this, my audience began to change. Mixed in with the horse owners and trainers and riders I saw more and more people whose lives had nothing directly to do with horses. I saw a lot of teachers — in fact, teachers were often the first people to understand what I was driving at. I even did a couple of lectures at teachers' conventions. I told them the same things I'd been saying all along. I told them that their attitude towards themselves was reflected in their attitude toward the horse. I told them that if it was their goal to teach the horse to trust and respect them, then they too would have to learn how to demonstrate trust and respect. I told them that if they wanted to control the horse, they had to be prepared to take the responsibility as well as the power. I showed them that the horse could help them learn these things. Although it was the same talk I gave to the horse people, the message crossed over to the teachers right away. What they always told me in return was, "It's just like teaching kids!"

Social workers and therapists were starting to come to the demonstrations, too. One day a man walked up to me after a clinic, introduced himself as Bob Friedrich, and then told me he'd read my book and went on to lay out an interesting proposition. Bob worked for the social services department of the Canadian government and he asked me if I'd put on a workshop for a group of social workers. I said I would, and soon after I found myself working a horse in a round pen before a group of social workers and their clients, young people who were having problems. Some of them were street kids. I worked with the horse for a while and then asked if any of the kids wanted to get in with me and see if they could establish a bond with the horse. One boy who looked about 15 was just shining with desire, so I opened the gate and ushered the little tough guy in. I coached him, and before long he figured it out. He found the right balance of assertiveness and restraint and he was able to control the horse without scaring it. After the session, a TV reporter asked the boy how he'd felt when he'd gotten the balance right. The kid beamed up at him: "It's the first time in my life I've been able to get what I wanted without having to start a fight for it." (Incidentally, I checked in with Bob about a year later and he told me that same young man was now off of the streets, he'd made great strides, was doing really well, and he actually had a job working in a horse barn.)

At a clinic in Orlando, Florida, I met and worked with a man named Michael McClain. Michael works for a large NASA contractor responsible for launching and processing the space shuttle. Michael's job is to co-ordinate and communicate between different departments and he's used to translating ideas from one context to another. He thought that what he'd learned while working with his horse that weekend was also valuable to his colleagues. Respect, trust and clear communication are always big issues in any workplace, too. The ideas we talked about soon began appearing in the company newsletter he wrote and he tells me that his co-workers really responded wonderfully to the predator-prey message.

Then there's my friend Ronnie from Sacramento, California. Ronnie's a firefighter, and he was a good one, too, until he was leading a group of men through the zero visibility of a burning house filled with thick smoke, searching for the owners they believed were trapped some-where inside, when the roof suddenly caved in on them. Fortunately, Ronnie was not too badly burned, but aside from believing he was about to die a horrible death, the worst of it was that at first, Ronnie had heard the other firemen screaming, and then they suddenly stopped, and he was overwhelmed with the thought that these brave men, his friends, had just died in the cave-in. Even though he was rescued and soon learned that everyone had actually gotten out safely, Ronnie never got over the overwhelming guilt and fear he'd felt when he thought his two comrades had died on his watch. After all, it had been his call to go in.

Later, Ronnie couldn't work anywhere near a fire and ended up on disability leave to heal, physically and mentally. He needed, but was resistant to, a heavy course of mainstream therapy. Ronnie loves horses, too, and he trains colts as a hobby. I joined him in his round pen for a couple of sessions and I could see he was struggling with something inside. We went out for a beer after the second session. He looked at me, shook his head and sighed. "Working in the round pen with that horse of mine pushes more buttons in me than when I go into my therapist's office," he said. One day, a friend shot some video of Ronnie and a horse. Watching himself, Ronnie realized how clearly his body spoke of stress seething under the surface. That realization was Ronnie's first step forward toward real health and now he's doing great. Ronnie is a hero to me because he is walking, talking proof that what doesn't kill us can only make us stronger if we have the humility, courage and determination to go forward.

Clearly, some link between horses and the human psyche was surfacing. And in the fall of 1998, I got my first e-mail from Dr. Jane. Jane MacNaughton is a medical doctor, who works hard as a family psychotherapist at her practice in Kingston, Ontario. Like most of us, she knows all too well how challenging it is to balance her career with her family and still find some quiet time for herself. She is married with three children and she's also a horse owner and rider. Sensing that something was missing from her relationship to her horse, she'd gone into a bookstore looking for something that would help her understand horse psychology. Struck by the title, she walked out with Horses Don't Lie. And before long, she was on the phone to me, asking if I had any interest in discussing the ties that might lie between horse work and therapy. I was very interested indeed. As it turned out, we had a lot to talk about.

In her practice, Dr. Jane often uses principles of Jungian therapy, a branch of psychoanalysis that tries to weave a balance between the outer world of action and events and the inner world of dream, fantasy and symbolism. A distinguishing feature of Jungian analysis is the concept of archetypes, symbols rising from the dark, deep psychic pool of the collective unconscious where humanity's common experience is stored. Archetypes express a complex of images and emotions that surround the defining experiences of human life. Examples include the Hero, the Divine Child, the Great Mother, Transformation, Death and Rebirth. They are the same for us all, no matter who we are or where we come from. It's as if they are built into the wiring of our brains. And one of the most commonly recurring archetypes is — you guessed it — the Horse.

We spent hours on the phone, Dr. Jane and I, comparing ideas and notes. We talked about what the Horse archetype has meant throughout the ages. It has been closely linked with our instinctive, primal drives. Jung thought the Horse's appearance could signify instincts out of control. The horse evokes intense feelings and unbridled passion instead of cool, collected thought. We also talked about some of the things I'd seen happen with horses and humans, things like the young boy's encounter with the horse when I'd done that clinic for the social workers. Dr. Jane could see benefits right away.

Issues around uncontrolled passions were constant in Dr. Jane's therapeutic practice and she asked me if I'd ever considered if horses might play a practical role in therapy. We knew we were on to something and even tossed around the idea of doing a series of joint lectures, but we lived so far apart it was tough to make anything happen. Then, in early 1999, I got an e-mail from a woman named Linda Myers.

Linda's son had picked up a copy of Horse's Don't Lie at a horse show and given it to her for Christmas. After reading it, she wanted to tell me about the Equine-Assisted Growth and Learning Association. EAGALA dates back to the early '90s and begins with a man named Greg Kersten. Greg grew up on a ranch and when he was a young boy, his father died. That led to a few difficult years and more than a few times, Greg skipped school. He used to hide out in the barn, tucking himself into the horse stalls. That's where he learned to read horse body language, the same place I did. Eventually, Greg became a counsellor, although his love of horses remained and he never lost his horsey ways. He used to come to work in a cowboy hat and boots, and some of the kids he worked with used to ask him about where he'd been. He'd promise to take them out to the ranch as a way to reward them for making progress. When he did, he noticed bringing the kids together with the horses always seemed to lead to more progress.

Then he got a call from Lynn Thomas, the director of the Aspen Ranch, a working cattle ranch that is also a youth treatment facility. She hired Greg to work at the ranch, and together the two of them started developing a series of techniques to bring horses together with the people who need their help. EAGALA was born soon after. Today, there are 400 certified EAGALA therapists in Canada and the U.S. — social workers, psychologists, psychiatrists and other professionals who have all taken the training pioneered by Greg and Lynn. One American college, Virginia Intermont College, offers a minor in equine-assisted therapy and several other colleges are considering it.

I was floored! Here I thought I was on my own and it turns out there's a whole school of thought moving in the same direction. It was just like when I started lecturing and was worried about being too far in front of my audience — when an idea's time is right, it suddenly and simultaneously appears all over the place like magic. And so many members in EAGALA had stories that echoed my experiences. Linda's is just one of them.

Linda had been working for years as a counsellor with troubled adolescents, but was growing increasingly discouraged. Nothing she was doing seemed to make any difference to the kids she had devoted her career to helping. They were impossible to reach, sealed off behind a curtain of evasions and mesmerized by drugs, booze, and a shallow, distraction-addicted culture. And their families didn't seem to care, at least not enough to commit to progressive change. The kids would leave her office just as sick as when they came in. Beaten down and disillusioned, Linda was ready to quit. She was going to chuck it in and become a realtor. Before she did, cancer intervened. Linda fought it successfully, but was forced to take a year off to recover. Linda had ridden horses as a little girl, and she returned to riding during her convalescence. She was amazed at the mental and physical healing effect it had on her, and when she returned to work she resolved to try and harness this tool for her clients. She became one of EAGALA's very first certified therapists and opened her new practice, complete with indoor riding arena, in October 1998.

Sherri was one of the first kids she worked with, one of a group of kids recovering from chemical dependencies. Sherri had also been sexually abused, and being victimised was common with her. One day, Linda was a bit late getting to the group session. When she walked in, several of the boys were holding Sherri upside down, teasing her and making sexual jokes at her expense. Linda stopped them, but the damage had been done. Sherri had been victimised again. She was at the bottom of the totem pole, everybody's butt.

Linda decided to try her newfound equine therapy skills and took the group to the round pen. Her goals were modest. She just wanted to get the group to work as a team to draw in and move the horse from one end of the arena to another. That's all she wanted, but she got quite a bit more.

Linda showed the kids how they could make a horse go forward by approaching its back end and make it stop by standing in front of it. When the boys tried it, they could all make the horse go but none of them could make it stop. They couldn't stand in front of the horse with enough confidence. The horse would keep moving forward and the bluffing boys eventually started backing up. None could stand their ground. But when Sherri tried it, she planted her little feet in the sand, held out her arms and chest and that was it. The horse couldn't move her. Instead, she moved the horse. She got so good she could push it all over the ring, all by herself. Nothing could have been more empowering, and that session was a turning point for her. Linda never took those kids back to her basement office again and they had many, many sessions together in the round pen. Sherri became a group leader. She learned to say "no" to the horse and "no" to her peers. She learned how to be assertive without being confrontational. She learned what a mutually consensual relationship felt like, and she transferred that to her everyday life. She learned she didn't have to be a victim.

I heard many such stories from EAGALA therapists. I was starting to have a few of my own, too. In many different situations and in many different ways, horses were enabling people to make contact with feelings they'd buried deep inside their shadow. There didn't seem to be any doubt that equine-assisted therapy worked. The question was, why? Linda believes that it works because horses are big and powerful and because they are so attuned to body language. Their size and sheer presence makes them impossible to ignore. A client may be able to tune out a counsellor droning on about taking charge of their life, but they can't tune out a 1,200 pound horse in the arena with them. Horses also give us a comforting familiarity, a safe reminder of all things basic, a primal memory and perhaps an ancestral connection to our grounding roots to Mother Nature. As well, working with the body helps you work with the spirit. At the very least, working with a horse will force you to look up. And as Dr. Joanne Moses, a remarkable therapist in Tucson, Arizona who has pioneered equine assisted psychotherapy says, "when you're dealing with a deeply depressed person, just getting them to look up is a major step forward." Finally, a horse gives you instant and honest feedback on what you're communicating."It's almost like the horse is a huge biofeedback mechanism," Linda says.

I think she's right about all those things. But I think there's more, that the reason horses can help us make such deep and profound changes in our lives is that they evoke something deep and profound in us. That something goes back to the conversations Dr. Jane MacNaughton and I were having. In our talks, we came to the conclusion that the horse offers us a powerful opportunity to reach inward and touch our deepest selves: When we get into the round pen, suddenly there's 1,200 pounds of prancing, snorting archetype right there in our face. Linda's right. We can't ignore a horse, any more than we can help what we feel when we stand in front of one. Horses, by embodying one of the deepest archetypes in our consciousness, most definitely stir us up. All those things that are buried away or girdled safely up start swirling around in our psyches.

After my talks with Dr. Jane, I came to believe that horses can be a direct connection into the unconscious. When we look at a horse, and especially when there's a horse strutting across the pen in front of us, we see the flesh-and-blood incarnation of powerful forces bottled up within us that we wish we had the guts to saddle and ride. These are the forces that Jung called the shadow self. We know those forces could take us to our dreams and turn us into our best selves. We also know those forces could destroy us. That's why we bottle them up in the first place. And when such hidden feelings are stirred-up and agitated, that's when we have the chance to work with them and learn to control them. Horses give us this opportunity. They do this to us whether we're aware of it or not. But what a powerful tool to be able to use consciously!

Carl Jung also talked a lot about life's paradox, and how important the embrace of seeming contradictions is as we travel the never-ending journey towards becoming fully human. Horses, which can both free us or hurt us, embody this paradox. How we handle this paradox in the arena becomes a metaphor for how we handle it everywhere. Only in this case, it's such a potent and direct metaphor, that we can use it to change reality. Horses force us to face our shadow selves. Once we do that, we discover much greater freedom as we go forward in life.

This, I believe, is where my next cycle will take me. I've spent years studying the how of horse-human com- munication and now it's clearly time to turn to the why. Fortunately, I've got lots of help. Friends and associates such as Dr. Jane and Linda continue to contribute much to my education. In return, I think I've been able to offer them the kind of thorough grounding in horse professionalism that the growing field of equine-assisted therapy needs. These therapists, after all, are coming from the clinical side. I've spent two decades getting to know horses inside out. We have much to give each other.

But I have other guides, too. Writers, thinkers and dreamers throughout history have returned frequently to the archetype of the horse and I look often to them. You don't have to go far to find examples. You can start with the Greek and Roman myths, as so much of our culture does. Those ancient and thought-provoking stories aren't just simple fantasies. They're shaped how they are for a reason, and they often give us powerful insights into our inner lives.

Take Neptune, the old Roman god of the sea who rides a chariot throughout his watery domain. Right there, you have two strong symbols of the unconscious, water and horses. Water is deep, formless and unchanging, like our subconscious, and the horse gives us, like Neptune, the power to move through it. It's up to us to harness our inner horses and direct the journey. I'm convinced that these ideas I've come across are not new concepts. They are in fact, some of the oldest ideas we have and I believe that the time is right to rediscover them. And as I travel and talk to people and show them what I've learned, I'm convinced that's what's happening. When I first started out on this path, I was afraid I wouldn't be taken seriously. Then, I was afraid I was the only person spreading this message. Both times I was wrong. People all over North America had come to the same conclusions I had and many others needed only a slight nudge to connect the dots. And all over North America, the evidence is pouring in that these ideas do indeed work.

Before I began my current life of lecturing and demonstrating, I thought things would evolve differently for me than they have. I pictured myself on horseback, perfectly attuned to my mount and my inner self. We would ride over the prairie, free to explore the limits of the horse-human relationship. I now realize that vision, while beautiful, was incomplete. There weren't any other people in it and that wasn't the direction my life was heading at all. My life these days is full of people — Anita, Raven and Adler, of course, but also the dozens and hundreds of people who come to hear me talk and watch me work. Often, I walk away from the round pen after a public session with tears of joy streaming down my face after watching people discover something of themselves through the kind, patient help of a horse. And the best part about it is that those discoveries have nothing directly to do with me. With the help of a horse, people make these breakthroughs all on their own. I show them the door and every time, they walk through it on their own. So I'd like to change the picture I painted for you at the end of the last chapter.

The next cycle of my life isn't going to be about galloping over the hills in solitude or dozing on the grassland while my horse grazes gently nearby. I'll still be on horseback, but now I imagine myself riding over to a neighbour's house. We chat, and then they saddle up with me and we ride off to the next home on the prairie. They join us too, and it goes on like that until we've got a whole string of horses and riders confidently riding off to explore uncharted territory. There's lots of talk and laughter. The horses hold themselves relaxed and easy. We stop together and start together. We all know what our goal is and we all helped to set it. Nobody gets bossed around, but when decisions need to be made we know how to make them. We're all happy as we amble together through the shortgrass. And this, too, will be magic.